McDougal Littell

MODERN WORLD HISTORY

PATTERNS OF INTERACTION

Chapters in Brief

McDougal Littell

A DIVISION OF HOUGHTON MIFFLIN COMPANY

ISBN-13: 978-0-618-40997-6   ISBN-10: 0-618-40997-1

Printed in the United States of America.

6 7 8 9 - CKI - 09 08 07 06

To the Teacher

Chapters in Brief consists of summaries of each chapter in *Modern World History: Patterns of Interaction* to give you support and flexibility in teaching U.S. history to your students. Spanish translations of these summaries can be found in the booklet, **In–Depth Resources in Spanish** Also available are audio tapes of these chapter summaries in both English and Spanish.

ORGANIZATION

Each three-page chapter summary is organized in the same way: A brief overview, which states the central idea of the chapter, is followed by a summary of each section of the textbook. Each section summary, in turn, begins with a statement of a key idea to focus students' reading and to help them comprehend the large issues of the chapter. Review questions at the end reinforce key ideas in the chapter, and an Answer Key follows immediately.

USES

There are a variety of ways to use these summaries. Here are a few suggestions:

- **To preview a chapter.** Having students read the summary before they begin studying a chapter will give them a context for understanding the details provided in the chapter itself. Slow readers gain special help by such a previewing strategy.

- **To reinforce and summarize main ideas.** Because the chapter summaries distill information into large issues and major trends, they are a perfect medium for teaching students how to identify main ideas in their reading.

- **To accommodate time constraints.** If it is not possible to cover every chapter in detail in the course of a semester or a school year, these chapter summaries offer a way to highlight chapters that may otherwise get skipped. Teachers using block schedules are especially grateful for these time-saving measures.

- **To review a chapter.** After students have read a chapter, they can use the summary to review key ideas, events, and people before taking the chapter test.

CHAPTERS IN BRIEF *The Rise of Democratic Ideas*

CHAPTER OVERVIEW *The ancient Greeks established the first democracy, while the Romans contributed to the development of democratic law. The Judeo-Christian tradition promoted ideas of social responsibility, individual worth, and equality. The rights of individuals and the power of Parliament increased over time in England. Enlightenment ideas influenced the American and French revolutions. The struggle for democracy continues to this day.*

❶ The Legacy of Ancient Greece and Rome

KEY IDEA *The first democracy, which was limited, developed in Athens. The Romans developed key principles of law and a written legal code.*

Ancient Greece was made up of city-states. The first democracy developed in the city-state of Athens.

At first, Athens had a king. Then, it became an aristocracy, a state ruled by the noble class. In the 6th century B.C., the leader Solon created four new kinds of citizenship. All free adult males were citizens, and all citizens were able to vote in the assembly, or governmental body. Citizens of the three higher classes could also hold public office. Still, democracy in Athens was limited. Officially, only about one-tenth of the population were citizens. Women, slaves, and foreign residents could not be citizens. Slaves made up about one-third of the Athenian population.

About one hundred years after Solon, a leader named Cleisthenes increased the power of the assembly. He allowed all citizens to submit laws for debate and passage. He also created a council consisting of people chosen at random.

During the Golden Age of Greece, Pericles strengthened democracy by increasing the number of paid public officials. This allowed poorer citizens to serve in government. He also introduced the idea of direct democracy, in which citizens participate directly in government rather than by means of people who represent them.

The Golden Age lasted less than 50 years. War and invasion brought the end of democracy. Respect for reason didn't die, however. The philosophers Socrates, Plato, and Aristotle examined beliefs and set forth new visions of government and society.

As Greece fell, Rome began to rise. By 509 B.C. Rome was a republic. A republic is a form of government in which citizens have the right to vote and to select their leaders. In Rome, as in Athens, however, citizenship with voting rights belonged only to males who were not born slaves.

Rome's republican government had separate branches. The legislative branch consisted of a Senate and two assemblies. Although the Senate was aristocratic, the assemblies were more democratic.

Rome's laws have influenced democracy. Some of the most important laws were

- All citizens have the right to equal treatment under the law.
- A citizen is considered innocent until proven guilty.
- The burden of proof rests with the accuser rather than the accused.
- A person is punished only for actions, not for thoughts.
- Any law that seemed unreasonable or grossly unfair could be set aside.

In 451 B.C. the Romans created the Twelve Tables. It gave all citizens the right to the protection of the law. About 1,000 years later, the extensive Code of Justinian was developed. Its many provisions became a guide on legal matters throughout western Europe. The Code established the idea of "a government of laws, not of men."

❷ The Judeo-Christian Tradition

KEY IDEA *Both Judaism and Christianity emphasized the worth of the individual and social responsibility. The Reformation and Renaissance further promoted ideas of individual worth..*

The Hebrews were the ancient people who developed Judaism. According to the Hebrew holy book, which is the Christian Old Testament, the Hebrews are the children of God. This Hebrew belief and others led to a new emphasis on the worth of the individual.

The Hebrews, also known as the Jews, had a written code of law. It was the Ten Commandments. God gave these laws to Moses in about 1200 B.C. These laws focused more on morality and ethics than they did on politics.

The Hebrews believed in acting responsibly toward others. They believed that the community should help the unfortunate. The prophets of Judaism hoped for a world without poverty or injustice.

Jesus was born in approximately 6 to 4 B.C. At age 30, he began preaching Jewish ideas, including the Ten Commandments. He also stressed the importance of people's love for God, their neighbors, their enemies, and themselves.

In the first century after Jesus' death, his followers started a new religion based on his messages. It was called Christianity. The apostle Paul spread this faith. He preached a message of equality. Equality of all human beings is an idea central to democracy.

By the Middle Ages, the Roman Catholic Church was the most powerful institution in Europe. During the Renaissance, people began to question the church. This questioning led to the Reformation. The Reformation was a protest movement against the power of the church. It was a call for change.

In Germany, Martin Luther criticized the church for selling pardons for sins. He also contradicted the church teachings that people were saved by grace and good works. Luther said people were saved only through faith in god. Soon, many new Protestant faiths sprang up.

Protestant ideas strengthened the idea of the importance of the individual. In Protestant faiths, the clergy did not have special powers. People could find their own way to God. They could read and interpret the Bible for themselves.

The Reformation broke apart the religious unity of Europe. It challenged the authority of Catholic monarchs and popes. It contributed to the growth of democracy.

❸ Democratic Developments in England

KEY IDEA *The Glorious Revolution completed a quest for democracy that began in the 12th century.*

An early democratic development in England was a form of trial by jury. It began in the 12th century.

Another early democratic development in England was "common law". Unlike Roman law, which expressed will of the ruler or lawmaker, common law reflected customs and principles established over time. Common law became the basis of the legal systems in many English-speaking countries, including the United States.

When King John became involved in a conflict with the English nobles in 1215, they presented their demands in the Magna Carta. This document contained important principles that tended to limit the power of the English monarch. One of the Magna Carta's 63 clauses said taxes could only be raised by the "common consent of our kingdom." Another clause had to do with the right to a jury trial and the protection of the law. This right is called due process of law.

In 1295, Edward I needed money to pay for a war. He called together all the lords, plus some knights and leading citizens of the towns. They helped Edward make decisions. This gathering was known as the Model Parliament. Parliament increasingly saw itself as a partner of the monarch in governing. Over time, its power also grew. It voted on taxes, passed laws, and advised on royal policies.

In the 16th century, monarchs began claiming greater authority. When they insisted on their divine right, or God-given right to rule, conflicts arose. In particular, Parliament clashed with James I. When James's son, Charles, became king, Parliament tried to limit royal power by forcing him to accept the Petition of Right. The petition, written in 1628, is a landmark in constitutional history. It demanded an end to

- Taxing without Parliament's consent
- Imprisoning citizens illegally
- Housing troops in citizen's homes
- Military government in peacetime

Although Charles signed the petition, he later ignored the promises he made. The English Civil War broke out between supporters of the king and his opponents. Charles was executed in 1649.

After a brief rule by Oliver Cromwell, a new Parliament restored the monarchy to England. Things had changed, however. The monarch could not tax without Parliament's consent. In addition, *habeas corpus* prevented authorities from wrongly or unjustly detaining a person.

A few years later, when Parliament withdrew its

support from King James, the Glorious Revolution began. As a result, England became a constitutional monarchy. In a constitutional monarchy, a ruler's powers are controlled by a constitution and the laws of the country.

In 1689, the king and queen accepted a bill of rights from Parliament. It limited the power of the monarchy. Democratic protections included free speech in Parliament, and no taxation without the consent of Parliament.

❹ The Enlightenment and Democratic Revolutions

KEY IDEA *Enlightenment ideas influenced the American and French revolutions. Struggles for democracy continue to this day.*

In the 17th and 18th centuries, an intellectual movement called the Enlightenment developed. Thinkers of this movement built their ideas around the earlier Greek philosophers' ideas of natural law. They hoped to use reason to discover the natural laws that govern society. They hoped to apply the scientific method to human affairs.

One Enlightenment thinker, Thomas Hobbes, decided the best form of government was absolute monarchy. He said people should form a type of social contract in which they submit to their ruler in order to prevent disorder. John Locke took a different view. He said all people had natural rights to life, liberty, and property. He said people form governments in order to protect these natural rights. He also said people have a right to rebel against a government that does not protect their rights. His ideas about government became the cornerstone of modern democratic thought.

French Enlightenment thinkers included Voltaire, Rousseau, and Montesquieu. Voltaire fought for tolerance, freedom of religion, and free speech. Rousseau called for direct democracy. He said the only legitimate government came from the consent of the governed. Montesquieu said that liberty was best safeguarded by dividing government into three branches: a law-making body, an executive branch, and courts.

Enlightenment ideas and British traditions influenced American colonists. They opposed British efforts to tax them without representation. They issued a Declaration of Independence on July 4, 1776. Locke's ideas strongly influenced this declaration.

Enlightenment ideas also shaped the American Constitution. The Constitution included a representative government and a federal system. In a federal system, powers of government are divided between the federal, or central, and state governments. The Constitution also separated powers, into to three branches, based on Montesquieu's ideas.

Near the end of the 18th century, revolution also occurred in France. The peasants were hungry and restless, and the middle class was dissatisfied with Louis XVI's government. In 1789 the commoners formed a National Assembly. It made many reforms. It adopted the Declaration of the Rights of Man and of the Citizen. This document guaranteed the rights of liberty, property, security, and resistance to oppression to all people. The Assembly also ended feudalism in France, drafted a constitution that made France a limited monarchy, and made many other reforms.

The work of the Assembly did not last long. A radical legislature took charge, and a reign of terror followed. Napoleon Bonaparte assumed control of France and created a dictatorship. Democracy in France did not develop until much later in the 1800s.

Today, the struggle for democracy goes on in various places around the world. The United Nations promotes this quest. Its Universal Declaration of Human Rights, adopted in 1948, states the right to life, liberty, and the security of person. It also includes rights to equal protection under law, to freedom of movement, and to freedom to assemble.

Recent struggles for democracy have occurred in the newly created republics of the former Soviet Union, and in East Timor. While democracy may be difficult to achieve and preserve, the desire for it remains constant.

Review

1. *Summarizing* Describe changes in democracy over time in Athens.
2. *Analyzing Cause and Recognizing Effect* Why were Roman developments in law so important?
3. *Determining the Main Ideas* How did the Judeo-Christian tradition contribute to the development of democracy?
4. *Determining the Main Ideas* How did the role of Parliament change over time in England?
5. *Evaluationg Courses of Action* Why do some democratic revolutions, like the one in the United States, succeed, while others fail?

Answer Key
Prologue
SUMMARY

The Rise of Democratic Ideas

Responses will vary but should include points similar to the following:

1. First Athens had a king; then it was an aristocracy. In the 6th century B.C., Solon created four kinds of citizenship. (Yet only a tenth of the population was citizens.) Cleisthenes extended democracy by increasing the power of the assembly. Pericles introduced the idea of direct democracy.

2. Roman laws influenced democracy in the Western world because they protected the rights of individuals. Many Roman laws are in force today.

3. The Judeo-Christian tradition introduced and spread ideas of social responsibility, the end of injustice, and equality before God.

4. Over the years, Parliament became more and more powerful. At first it was a group that could be summoned (or not) at the king's whim. Then it began to assume a partnership in governing. Finally, it significantly limited the power of the monarchy and, together with the laws of the country, assumed authority.

5. Democratic revolutions may fail because they do not put into place far-seeing laws or protections for citizens. They may not tolerate dissent. They may occur too quickly without enough planning. Once in power, new democratic leaders may lose their democratic vision.

CHAPTER 1

Summary

CHAPTERS IN BRIEF *European Renaissance and Reformation, 1300–1600*

CHAPTER OVERVIEW *In the 1300s, a renewed interest in classical learning and the arts arose in Italy. Thinkers in northern Europe adopted these ideas as well but with a spiritual focus. The desire for a more satisfying spiritual life led some to revolt against the Catholic Church, as new churches were founded. In response, the Catholic Church undertook some reforms of its own, strengthening the faith.*

❶ Italy: Birthplace of the Renaissance

KEY IDEA *The European Renaissance, a rebirth of learning and the arts, began in Italy in the 1300s.*

The years 1300 to 1600 saw a rebirth of learning and culture in Europe. Called the Renaissance, it spread north from Italy. It began there for three reasons. First, Italy had several important cities, whereas most of northern Europe was still rural. Second, these cities included a class of merchants and bankers who were becoming wealthy and powerful. Third, Italian artists and scholars were inspired by the ruined buildings and other reminders of classical Rome.

That new interest in the classical past led to an important value in Renaissance culture—humanism. This was a deep interest in what people have already achieved as well as what they could achieve in the future. Scholars did not try to connect classical writings to Christian teaching but tried to understand them on their own terms. Renaissance thinkers stressed the things of the world. In the Middle Ages, the emphasis had been mostly on spiritual values. One way that powerful or wealthy people showed this interest in worldly things was by paying artists, writers, and musicians to create beautiful works of art.

Men tried to show that they could master many fields of study or work. Someone who succeeded in many fields was admired greatly. The artist Leonardo da Vinci was an example of this ideal. He was a painter, a scientist, and an inventor. Men were expected to be charming, witty, well-educated, well-mannered, athletic, and self-controlled. Women were expected not to create art but to inspire artists.

Renaissance artists sometimes used new methods. Sculptors made figures more realistic than those from the Middle Ages. Painters used perspective to create the illusion that their paintings

were three-dimensional. The subject of artwork changed also. Art in the Middle Ages was mostly religious, but Renaissance artists reproduced other views of life. Michelangelo showed great skill as an architect, a sculptor, and a painter.

Renaissance writers reached high achievements as well. Several wrote in their native languages, whereas most writing in the Middle Ages had been in Latin. Writers also changed their subject matter. They wrote to express their own thoughts and feelings or to portray in detail an individual. Dante and others wrote poetry, letters, and stories that were self-expressive and more realistic. Niccolò Machiavelli took a new approach to understanding government. He focused on telling rulers how to expand their power, even if that meant taking steps that the Church might view as evil.

❷ The Northern Renaissance

KEY IDEA *In the 1400s, northern Europeans began to adopt the ideas of the Renaissance.*

By 1450, the bubonic plague had ended in northern Europe and the population was recovering. Also, the Hundred Years' War between France and England was ending. The suffering caused by these two events was fading, and the new ideas from Italy spread to northern Europe, where they were quickly adopted. The northern Renaissance had a difference, however. While the educated people there became interested in classical learning, they were more likely to combine that with interest in religious ideas.

Major artists appeared in parts of Germany, France, Belgium, and the Netherlands. The use of oil-based paints became popular. Dürer painted religious subjects and realistic landscapes. Holbein, van Eyck, and Bruegel painted lifelike portraits and scenes of peasant life. They revealed much about the times.

The new ideas of Italian art moved to the north, where artists began to use them. Painters in Flanders were deeply interested in showing life in realistic ways. They painted members of the rising merchant class and peasants, revealing much about life of the period. One pioneered in the use of oil-based paints.

Writers of the northern Renaissance combined humanism with deep Christian faith. They urged reforms in the Church and society to try to make people more devoted to God and more just. Thomas More wrote a book about an imaginary ideal society where greed, war, and conflict did not exist.

William Shakespeare is widely viewed as the greatest playwright of all time. His plays showed a brilliant command of the English language and a deep understanding of people and how they interact with one another.

One reason that learning spread so rapidly during the Renaissance was the invention of movable type. The Chinese had invented the process of carving characters onto wooden blocks. They then arranged them in words, inked the blocks, and pressed them against paper to print pages. In 1440, a German, Johann Gutenberg, adopted this practice. He produced his first book—a Bible—in 1455. The technology then spread rapidly. By 1500, presses in Europe had printed nearly 10 million books.

Printing made it easier to make many copies of a book. As a result, written works became available far and wide. Fewer books were printed in Latin, and more books were printed in languages such as English, French, Spanish, Italian, or German. As a result, more people began to read the Bible on their own. Some formed ideas about Christianity that differed from those of the Church.

❸ Luther Leads the Reformation

KEY IDEA *Martin Luther's protest over abuses in the Catholic Church led to the founding of Protestant churches.*

By 1500, Renaissance values emphasizing the individual and worldly life weakened the influence of the Church. At the same time, many people sharply criticized the Church for some of its practices. Popes seemed more concerned with luxury and political power than with spiritual matters. Critics resented the fact that they paid taxes to support the Church in Rome. The lower clergy had

faults. Many local priests lacked education and couldn't teach people. Others took actions that broke their vows as priests.

In the past, reformers had urged that the Church change its ways to become more spiritual and humble. Christian humanists such as Erasmus and More added their voices to calls for change. In the early 1500s, the calls grew louder.

In 1517, a German monk and professor named Martin Luther protested some actions of a Church official. That person was selling what were called indulgences. By paying money to the Church, people thought they could win salvation. Luther challenged this practice and others. He posted a written protest on the door of a castle church. His words were quickly printed and began to spread throughout Germany. Thus began the Reformation, the movement for reform that led to the founding of new Christian churches.

Soon Luther pushed for broader changes. He said that people could win salvation only through faith, not good works. He said that religious beliefs should be based on the Bible alone and that the pope had no real authority. He said that each person was equal before God. He or she did not need a priest to explain the Bible to them.

The pope punished Luther for his views, but he refused to take them back. The Holy Roman Emperor, a strong Catholic, called Luther an outlaw. His books were to be burned. No one was to shelter him. Meanwhile, many of his ideas were being put into practice. The Lutheran Church was born around 1522.

In 1524, peasants in Germany hoped to use Luther's ideas to change society. They demanded an end to serfdom—a condition like slavery. When it was not granted, they revolted. Luther disagreed with this revolt, and the German princes killed thousands in putting the revolt down. Some nobles supported Luther because they saw a chance to weaken the emperor's power. German princes joined forces against Luther. Some princes protested this. War broke out between Catholics and these Protestant forces in Germany. It finally ended in 1555 with the Peace of Augsburg. That treaty granted each prince the right to decide whether his subjects would be Catholic or Protestant.

The Catholic Church faced another challenge to its power in England. Henry VIII, the king, was married to a princess of Spain. She had borne him a daughter, but he wanted a son. This could prevent a civil war erupting when he died. His wife was too old to have another child, but the pope refused to grant him a divorce. In 1534, Henry had the English Parliament pass a number of laws that took England out of the Catholic Church. The laws made the king or queen, not the pope, head of the Church of England. Henry remarried four times, gaining his only son from his third wife.

One of Henry's daughters, Elizabeth, became queen in 1558 and completed the task of creating a separate English church. New laws gave the new religion some traits that would appeal to both Protestants and Catholics. In this way, Elizabeth hoped to end religious conflict in England.

❹ The Reformation Continues

KEY IDEA *John Calvin and other Reformation leaders begin new Protestant churches. The Catholic Church also made reforms.*

Protestantism arose elsewhere in the 1530s under the leadership of John Calvin. Calvin wrote an important book that gave structure to Protestant beliefs. He taught that people are sinful by nature and only those God chooses—"the elect"—will be saved. He said that God knew from the beginning which people would be saved and which would not.

Calvin created a government run by religious leaders in a city in Switzerland. The city had strict rules of behavior that urged people to live deeply religious lives. Anyone who preached different religious ideas might be burned at the stake.

A preacher named John Knox was impressed by Calvin's high moral ideals. Knox put these ideas into practice in Scotland. This was the beginning of the Presbyterian Church. Others in Switzerland, Holland, and France adopted Calvin's ideas as well. In France, his followers were called Huguenots. Conflict between them and Catholics often turned to violence. In 1572, mobs killed about 12,000 Huguenots. Another Protestant church that arose was the Anabaptists. They preached that people should be baptized into the faith as adults. They influenced some later groups.

Protestant churches grew, but millions remained true to the Catholic faith. Still, the Catholic Church took steps to reform itself. A Spanish noble named Ignatius founded a new group in the Church based on deep devotion to Jesus. Members started schools across Europe. They tried to convert people to

Catholicism who were not Christians. In addition, they tried to stop the spread of Protestant faiths in Europe.

Two popes of the 1500s helped bring about changes in the Church. Paul III took several steps, including calling a great council of church leaders at Trent, in northern Italy. The council, which met in 1545, passed these doctrines:

- the Church's interpretation of the Bible was final;
- Christians needed good works as well as faith to win salvation;
- the Bible and the Church had equal authority in setting out Christian beliefs; and
- indulgences could be sold.

Paul also put in action a kind of court called the Inquisition. It was charged with finding, trying, and punishing people who broke the rules of the Church. His successor, Paul IV, put these policies into practice. These actions helped revive the Church and allowed it to survive the challenge of the Protestants.

Review

1. *Analyzing Causes and Recognizing Effects* Why did the Renaissance arise in Italy?
2. *Making Inferences* Why do you think that a person who is accomplished in many fields is called a "Renaissance" man or woman?
3. *Contrasting* How did the northern Renaissance differ from the Italian Renaissance?
4. *Drawing Conclusions* What role did political concerns play in the Reformation?
5. *Forming and Supporting Opinions* Which leader—Calvin or Luther—do you think had a greater impact? Explain why.

Answer Key
Chapter 1
SUMMARY

European Renaissance and Reformation, 1300–1600

Responses will vary but should include points similar to the following:

1. The Renaissance arose in Italy because of the strong element of city life, the merchants who had wealth and power, and the presence of reminders of ancient classical heritage.

2. Such a person is called a "Renaissance" man or woman because to be accomplished in many fields was an ideal of the Renaissance.

3. The northern Renaissance was more interested in spiritual matters along with classical studies than was the Italian Renaissance.

4. Some German princes backed Luther's ideas because they wanted to weaken the power of the emperor, who was Catholic. Also, Henry VIII's desire to have a son—and avoid a possible civil war—led to the break between the English church and Catholicism.

5. Luther launched the Reformation, but Calvin's ideas had impact on the Protestant churches of many different countries.

CHAPTER 2

Summary

CHAPTERS IN BRIEF *The Muslim World Expands, 1300–1700*

CHAPTER OVERVIEW *A group of Turks called Ottomans set up a new empire in what is now modern Turkey. Farther to the east, the Safavid Empire arose in modern Iran, where rulers embraced a special type of Islam that made them different from their neighbors. Meanwhile, India saw the rise of yet another empire as Muslims created a powerful state there.*

❶ The Ottomans Build a Vast Empire

KEY IDEA *The Ottomans established a Muslim Empire that combined many cultures and lasted for more than 600 years.*

In 1300, the world of the eastern Mediterranean was seeing changes. The Byzantine Empire was fading. The Seljuk Turk state had been destroyed by the Mongols. Anatolia, the area of modern Turkey, was now inhabited by groups of nomadic Turks. They saw themselves as ghazis, or warriors for Islam. They formed military groups and raided the lands where non-Muslims lived.

The most successful ghazi was Osman. Western Europeans took his name to be Othman and called his followers Ottomans. Between 1300 and 1326, Osman built a strong but small kingdom in Anatolia. Leaders who came after Osman called themselves sultans, or "ones with power." They extended the kingdom by buying land, forming alliances with other chieftains, and conquering everyone they could. The military success of the Ottomans was aided by gunpowder—especially as used in cannons.

The Ottomans ruled kindly through local officials appointed by the sultan. Muslims had to serve in the army but paid no taxes. Non-Muslims paid the tax but did not have to serve in the army. Many joined Islam simply to avoid the tax. Most people in their empire adjusted quickly to their easy rule.

One warrior did not. Timur the Lame, called Tamerlane in the west, arose in central Asia. He claimed to be descended from Genghis Khan. The claim probably is not true—but he was as fierce as the Mongol conqueror. He conquered Russia and Persia, where he burned the city of Baghdad to the ground. In 1402, he defeated the Ottomans in battle and captured the sultan. Timur died three years later on his way to conquer China.

Back in Anatolia, the four sons of the last sultan fought for control of the empire. Mehmed I won

control, and his son and the four following sultans brought the Ottoman Empire to its greatest power. One of them—Mehmed II—took power in 1451 and captured Constantinople. At first, his ships were unable to sail near the city because barriers blocked the way. So he had his soldiers drag the ships over hills so they could be launched on another side of Constantinople. After several weeks of fighting, the Ottoman force was simply too strong for the tiny army left in the city. In 1453, Constantinople finally fell to the Ottomans. Mehmed made the city his capital, which was renamed Istanbul. The famous and beautiful church of the Hagia Sophia became a mosque. The rebuilt city became home to people from all over the Ottoman Empire.

Other emperors used conquest to make the empire grow. After 1514, Selim the Grim took Persia, Syria, and Palestine. He then captured Arabia, took the Muslim holy cities of Medina and Mecca, and gained control of Egypt.

His son, Suleyman I, brought the Ottoman Empire to its greatest size and most impressive achievements. He conquered parts of southeastern Europe by 1525. He won control of the entire eastern Mediterranean Sea and took North Africa as far west as Tripoli. Although he was defeated in a battle for Vienna in 1529, his Ottoman Empire remained huge.

Suleyman ruled his empire with a highly structured government. Serving the royal family and the government were thousands of slaves. Among them was an elite group of soldiers called janissaries. They were Christians taken as children and made slaves with personal loyalty to the sultan. They were trained as soldiers and fought fiercely for the sultan. Other slaves held important government jobs. The empire allowed people to follow their own religion. Jews and Christians were not mistreated by the Ottomans. Suleyman revised the laws of the empire, which won him the name Suleyman the Lawgiver. Suleyman also oversaw an empire that was full of accomplished works of art. Using an excellent architect, he built many fine buildings in his capital.

The empire lasted long after Suleyman but spent the next few hundred years in decline. None of the sultans were as accomplished as he had been, and the Ottoman Empire's power slipped.

❷ Cultural Blending Case Study: The Safavid Empire

KEY IDEA *Many world cultures incorporate influences from various peoples and traditions.*

Throughout history, different peoples have lived together, and their cultures have influenced one another. Often these people have blended one culture with another. This can be due to trade, conquest, movement of people from one area to another, or conversion to a new religion.

Changes often happen in places where cultural blending takes place. Changes in language, arts and architecture or religion are examples. For example in the Safavid empire the spoken language was Persian. But after Muslims came to live in the empire, Arabic words appeared in the Persian language.

Cultural blending took place in the Safavid Empire of Persia. The Safavids began as members of an Islamic group that claimed to be related to the prophet Muhammad. In the 1400s, they became allied with the Shi'a, a branch of Islam. The major group of Muslims, the Sunnis, persecuted the Shi'a for their views. The Safavids, fearing their strong neighbors who were Sunni Muslims, decided to build a strong army to protect themselves.

In 1499, a 14-year-old leader named Isma'il led this army to conquer Iran. He took the traditional Persian title of shah, or king, and made the new empire a state of Shi'a. He destroyed Baghdad's Sunni population. Ottoman Turk rulers—who were Sunni Muslims—in turn killed all the Shi'a that they met. This conflict between the two groups of Muslims continues today.

The Safavids reached their height in the late 1500s under Shah Abbas. He reformed the military, making two armies that were loyal to him and him alone. He also gave new weapons to the army to make them better fighters. He reformed the government, getting rid of corrupt officials. He also brought gifted artists to his empire, who helped make his capital and other cities very beautiful. In

taking these steps, Shah Abbas drew on good ideas from other cultures. He used Chinese artists and enjoyed good relations with nations of Europe. Through this contact, the demand for Persian rugs increased greatly in Europe. In this period, rug-making, which had simply been a local craft in Persia, was changed into a major industry for the country.

As with the Ottoman Empire, the Safavid Empire began to decline soon after it had reached its greatest height. Shah Abbas had killed or injured his most talented sons—just as Suleiman had done—fearing that they would seize power from him. As a result, a weak and ineffective grandson became shah after him. Under his poor leadership, the empire lost power.

While the empire fell, the blended culture that the Safavid Empire had created continued. The main elements of that culture were the joining together of the Persian tradition of learning and sophistication and the devout faith of the Shi'a. These elements are found in Iran even today.

❸ The Mughal Empire in India

KEY IDEA *The Mughal Empire brought Turks, Persians, and Indians together in a vast empire.*

Starting in the 600s, India went through a long period of unsettled life and trouble. After the Gupta Empire fell, nomads from central Asia invaded the area and created many small kingdoms. In the 700s, Muslims arrived on the scene. Their arrival launched a long history of fighting between them and the Hindus who had lived in India for centuries.

The Hindus were able to prevent the Muslims from taking their land for about 300 years. Then a group of Muslim Turks conquered a region around the city of Delhi and set up a new empire there. They treated the Hindus in their area harshly. Their rule ended in 1398, when Timur the Lame totally destroyed Delhi.

A little over a hundred years later, a new power arose. Babur had a small kingdom north of India. He raised an army and began to win large parts of India. Babur had many talents. He was a lover of poetry and gardens and a sensitive man who used his feelings for others to become a superb leader. He was also an excellent general. He once led a force of only 12,000 soldiers to victory over an enemy army of 100,000. His empire was called the Mughal

Empire because he and his families were related to the Mongols.

Babur's grandson, Akbar, was equally talented. His name means "Greatest One," and the name seems suitable to the man. He ruled with great wisdom and fairness for almost 40 years.

Akbar was a Muslim, but he believed strongly that people should be allowed to follow the religion they chose. He set an example by letting his wives practice whatever religion they chose. In his government, too, Akbar hired people based on their ability and not their religion. Both Hindus and Muslims gained jobs as government workers.

Akbar ruled fairly. He ended the tax that Hindu pilgrims had to pay. He also ended the tax that all non-Muslims had to pay. To raise money, he imposed a tax based on a percentage of the food grown. This made it easier for peasants to pay the tax. His land policy was less wise. He generously gave land to government officials. However, when they died he took it back and handed it to someone else. As a result, workers did not see any point in caring for the land because they were not preserving it for their children.

He had a strong, well-equipped army that helped him win and maintain control of more lands. His empire held about 100 million people—more than lived in all of Europe at the time.

During Akbar's reign, many changes in culture took place. His policy of blending different cultures produced two new languages. Hindi blended Persian and local languages. It is still widely spoken in India today. Urdu grew out of a mixture of Arabic, Persian, and Hindi and was spoken by the soldiers in Akbar's camp. Today it is the official language of Pakistan. The empire became famous for its book illustrations, which were adapted from the art of Persia. Akbar—who could not read—had a huge library of books and served as a patron to many writers. He also sponsored the building of a new capital city and many buildings.

After Akbar's death in 1605, the empire began to decline. During the reign of Jahangir, the real power was his wife, Nur Jahan. She was an able ruler but had a bitter political battle with one of Jahangir's sons. Since that son found help from the Sikhs—members of a separate religion—that group became the target of attacks by the government.

Jahangir's successor was Shah Jahan, and he too chose not to follow Akbar's policy of religious toleration. Shah Jahan was a great patron of the arts and built many beautiful buildings, including the famous Taj Mahal. It was a tomb for his beloved wife. However, his ambitious building plans required high taxes, and the people suffered under his rule.

His son Aurangzeb ruled for almost 50 years and made the empire grow once again with new conquests. However, his rule brought about new problems. A serious Muslim, the new ruler put harsh new laws in place. He punished Hindus and destroyed their temples, which produced a rebellion that managed to take control of part of his empire. At the same time, the Sikhs had become skilled fighters, and they won control of another part of the empire. To fight these battles, Aurangzeb had to increase taxes. Since he only taxed Hindus, not Muslims, this move only made large numbers of people more and more angry.

After his death, the empire fell apart, and local leaders took control of small areas. There continued to be a Mughal emperor, but he was only a figurehead, not a ruler with any real power.

Review

1. *Clarifying* How did the Ottomans treat non-Muslims?
2. *Summary* What were Suleyman's major accomplishments?
3. *Determining Main Ideas* Despite their brilliant rule, what critical mistake did Suleiman and Shah Abbas make?
4. *Drawing Conclusions* What evidence of cultural blending can you find in Akbar's rule?
5. *Analyzing Causes and Recognizing Effects* How did Akbar's successors contribute to the end of the Mughal Empire?

Answer Key
Chapter 2
SUMMARY

The Muslim World Expands, 1300–1700

Responses will vary but should include points similar to the following:

1. The Ottomans treated non-Muslims well, allowing them to practice their own religion, although they did put a tax on them. They also placed some Christians into slavery, to serve as soldiers or government officials.

2. Suleyman brought the Ottoman Empire to its greatest size; revised the laws of the empire; had accomplished works of art and architecture created.

3. Both Suleiman and Shah Abbas weakened their empires by killing or hurting their sons who were able, leaving only weak rulers to follow them.

4. Akbar's policy of blending produced two new languages, Hindi and Urdu. The art of illustrating books, which became refined under his rule, was adapted from Persian art. He also gave government jobs to either Muslims or Hindus based on ability, not religion.

5. Akbar's successors did not continue his policy of religious toleration, which led to conflict between Hindus and Muslims. Ambitious building programs and military campaigns produced high taxes, which were unfairly paid only by Hindus. This added to the conflict between groups.

CHAPTER 3

Summary

CHAPTERS IN BRIEF *An Age of Exploration and Isolation, 1400–1800*

CHAPTER OVERVIEW *"God, glory, and gold" drove Europeans' early exploration of Asia. They took control of Asian trade, with Portugal leading the way. Eventually, nations of northern Europe displaced the Portuguese. Two dynasties in China resisted the growing power of Europeans in Asia, limiting Chinese contact with foreigners. In Japan, a new system of government brought peace and isolation.*

❶ Europeans Explore the East

KEY IDEA *Driven by the desire for wealth and to spread Christianity, Europeans began an age of exploration.*

For many centuries, Europeans had been largely, though not completely, isolated from contact with people from other lands. That changed in the 1400s. One reason for this change was that Europeans hoped to gain new sources of wealth. By exploring the seas far from Europe, traders hoped to find new, faster routes to Asia—the source of spices and luxury goods. Their goal was to win access to these lands and bypass the Muslims and Italians who currently controlled this trade. Another reason was the desire to spread Christianity to new lands. The Crusades had ended, but bad feelings between Christians and Muslims remained. The Christians of Europe wanted to convert the people of Asia.

Advances in technology made these voyages possible. A new kind of ship, the caravel, was stronger built than earlier ships. It had triangle-shaped sails that allowed it to sail against the wind. Ships could now travel far out into the ocean. The magnetic compass allowed sea captains to better stay on course.

The first nation to develop and use these new technologies was Portugal. Prince Henry of Portugal was deeply committed to the idea of exploring beyond the seas. In 1419, he started a school of navigation where sea captains, mapmakers, and navigators could meet, learn, and exchange ideas. Over the next few decades, Portuguese captains sailed farther and farther down the west coast of Africa. In 1488, Bartolomeu Dias led the first voyage to reach the southern tip of Africa. Ten years later, Vasco da Gama led a ship 27,000 miles around Africa, to India, and back. The Portuguese had found a sea route to Asia.

The Spanish, meanwhile, had plans of their own. Italian sailor Christopher Columbus convinced the king and queen that he could reach Asia by sailing west. In 1492, instead of landing in Asia, Columbus touched land in the islands of the Americas, land unknown to Europeans. At first, though, people still thought that he had landed in Asia. Spain and Portugal argued over which nation had the rights to the land that Columbus had claimed. In 1494, they signed the Treaty of Tordesillas. It divided the world into two areas. Portugal won the right to control the eastern parts and Spain the western parts—including most of the Americas.

Portugal moved quickly to make the new Indian Ocean route pay off. In 1509, it defeated a Muslim fleet off the coast of India and thus became the master of Indian trade. Soon, it captured cities in India and on the Malay peninsula. Portugal now had power over islands that were so rich in desirable spices that they were called the Spice Islands. Spices now cost Europeans one-fifth of what they had cost before, while still making Portugal very wealthy.

Other European nations joined in this trade. In the 1600s, the English and Dutch entered the East Indies to challenge Portugal. The Dutch fleet—about 20,000 ships—was the largest in the world. These two nations quickly broke Portuguese power in the area. Then both nations set up an East India Company to control Asian trade. These companies were more than businesses. They were like governments, with the power to make money, sign treaties, and raise their own armies. The Dutch managed to drive out the English and grab the Asian trade for themselves.

The Dutch made their trading headquarters on the island of Java in the East Indies. By 1700, the Dutch ruled much of Indonesia. They had trading posts in many other Asian countries and commanded the southern tip of Africa. At the same time, both England and France finally gained footholds in India.

While the Europeans controlled the trade between Asia and Europe, they had little impact on most people living in these areas. From 1500 to 1800, the people of Asia were largely untouched by the European traders.

❷ China Limits European Contacts

KEY IDEA *Advances under the Ming and Qing dynasties left China self-contained and uninterested in European contact.*

Mongol rule in China ended in 1368 when Hongwu led a rebel army that took control of the country. He declared himself the first emperor of the Ming Dynasty, which was to last for almost 300 years. Hongwu began his rule by increasing the amount of food produced, improving irrigation, and raising cotton and sugar cane. He also made changes that improved the government of China. Later he grew suspicious and untrusting. He caused the deaths of many people whom he suspected of plotting against him.

His son Yonglo continued his better policies and also launched a major effort at making contact with other Asian peoples. Beginning in 1405, an admiral named Zheng He led several voyages to Southeast Asia, India, Arabia, and Africa. The goal was to impress other people with the power and wealth of China. He also wanted to convince them to pay tribute to China each year. By sending gifts each year, these peoples would recognize that China was superior to them. Gifts did flow to China, but scholar-officials said that the voyages wasted valuable resources. Zheng He's journeys were stopped after seven years.

China allowed Europeans to trade officially at only three ports. China became isolated. However, illegal trade took place all along the coast. Because Europeans wanted Chinese silk and ceramics, the people began making large amounts of these goods. Europeans paid silver for them. Manufacturing never grew very large in China, however. The Confucian ideas that shaped Chinese thinking said that farming was a better way of life, so manufacturing was heavily taxed. European missionaries entered China at this time, bringing both Christianity and new technology.

The power of the Ming Dynasty declined because the government could not solve several problems. Rebels from Manchuria—a land to the north of China—took control of the country in 1644 and started a new dynasty called the Qing. At first, the Chinese people did not accept the new rulers, who were not Chinese. However, the Qing emperors won their support by taking steps to improve conditions in the country and by preserving Chinese traditions.

Two emperors were the most effective. Kangxi ruled from 1661 to 1721 and his grandson Qian-long served from 1736 to 1795. They brought China to its largest size, increased its wealth, and sponsored an increase in artistic production.

Qian-long had problems to face, however. One was the matter of trade. The Chinese insisted that Europeans had to follow certain rules in order to continue trading with them. The Dutch were willing to do so, and they carried on the largest share of trade with China. The British, though, did not agree to following these rules. This disagreement later led to conflict that broke up China's empire.

In China, the production of rice and the long period of peace gave the people better lives. In the 1600s and 1700s, the number of people in China almost doubled, rising to more than 300 million by 1800. The huge majority of these people were farmers. Because of the use of fertilizer and better irrigation, they could grow more food. They also began to grow new crops brought over from the Americas, such as corn and sweet potatoes. As a result, the level of nutrition improved, which led to the growth in population.

Women suffered in this period, however. Sons were valued over daughters. It was felt only sons could carry out family religious duties and tend to the family farm. For that reason, many infant girls were killed, and adult women were given few rights.

The invasions by the foreigners from Manchuria and the pressure from European traders bothered the Chinese. Artists created books and paintings that showed traditional Chinese values and ideas. Plays about Chinese history and heroes were popular. They helped to unify the Chinese people. At the same time, a feeling of national pride also was rising in neighboring Korea, a land that had long been dominated by China.

❸ Japan Returns to Isolation

KEY IDEA The Tokugawa regime unified Japan and began a 200-year period of isolation, autocracy, and economic growth.

From 1467 to 1568, Japan entered a long, dark period of civil war. Powerful warriors took control of large areas of land. They were called daimyo. They became the most important powers in the country in a feudal system similar to that of Europe's Middle Ages. The daimyo built strong castles. They also had small armies of samurai warriors on horses and soldiers on foot with guns. They fought each other constantly to gain more land for themselves.

In 1568, one of the daimyo took control of Kyoto, the site of the emperor's capital. He was unable to win complete control of Japan, however. Another general, Toyotomi Hideyoshi, continued the work of bringing all of Japan under one rule. Using military conquest and clever diplomacy, he won that goal in 1590. He failed in his effort to capture Korea, however, and died in 1598.

The work of unifying Japan was completed by Tokugawa Ieyasu, who became the shogun, or sole ruler. He moved the capital of Japan to a small fishing village named Edo. Later, it grew to become the city of Tokyo. While all of Japan was ruled by Tokugawa, the daimyo still held much power in their lands. Tokugawa solved that problem by forcing them to follow his orders. He required them to live every other year in his capital—and leave their families in the capital with him during the other years. As a result, no daimyo was able to rebel against his power. Tokugawa died in 1616. All of the shoguns to follow him were from his family. They maintained a strong central government in Japan. This system of rule, called the Tokugawa Shogunate, lasted until 1867.

The new government brought about a long period of peace and prosperity for most people. Peasant farmers suffered greatly during this time, however. They worked long and hard on the farms and paid heavy taxes. Many left the countryside to move to the cities. By the mid-1700s, Edo had more than a million people and was perhaps the largest city in the world. Women found more opportunities for work in this and other cities than they had in the country.

A traditional culture thrived. It preferred ceremonial Noh dramas, stories of ancient warriors, and paintings of classical scenes. However, in cities, new styles emerged. Townspeople attended kabuki theater dramas of urban life. They hung woodblock prints of city scenes in their homes.

Europeans began to arrive in Japan. In 1543, the Portuguese were first. They brought such goods as clocks, eyeglasses, and guns. Japanese merchants and the daimyo welcomed them at first. They even welcomed the Christian missionaries who came after 1549, hoping to convert the Japanese to Christianity.

Some missionaries scorned traditional Japanese beliefs, though. Tokugawa became worried. In 1612, he banned Christianity from the country. Over the next 20 years or so, Japan managed to rid the country of all Christians. This effort became part of a larger plan to protect the country from European influence. In 1639, leaders sealed Japan's borders except for one port city. It was open to only the Chinese and the Dutch. The Tokugawa shoguns controlled that port city, so they had tight control over all foreign contact. For the next 200 years, Japan remained closed to virtually all European contact.

Review

Analyzing Causes and Recognizing Effects

1. Why did the Europeans begin to explore overseas, and what technological changes made it possible?
2. Why did the Chinese stop the voyages of Zheng He?
3. What factors led to the growth in the Chinese population?
4. *Determining Main Ideas* What social changes took place in Tokugawa Japan?

Answer Key
Chapter 3
SUMMARY

An Age of Exploration and Isolation, 1400–1800

Responses will vary but should include points similar to the following:

1. Europeans began to explore overseas in search of wealth and converts to Christianity. Their voyages were made possible by a new, stronger ship design, triangular sails that allowed the ships to sail against the wind, and magnetic compasses that helped them stay on course.

2. The Chinese stopped the voyages of Zheng He because the emperor's scholar-officials said they were too costly.

3. The Chinese population grew because of better farming—due to use of fertilizer, better irrigation, and the introduction of crops from the Americas—and a long period of peace.

4. In Tokugawa Japan, the country became more urban and less rural. This development led to the creation of two separate cultures—the traditional culture and an urban-based culture.

CHAPTER

4

Summary

CHAPTERS IN BRIEF *The Atlantic World, 1492–1800*

CHAPTER OVERVIEW *Starting in 1492, the Spanish built a large empire in the Americas, but the native peoples suffered. In North America, the Dutch, French, and English fought for control. England finally won. The labor of enslaved persons brought from Africa supported the American colonies. The contact between the Old World and the New produced an exchange of new ideas.*

❶ Spain Builds an American Empire

KEY IDEA *The voyages of Columbus prompted the Spanish to carve out the first European colonies in the Americas.*

In 1492, Christopher Columbus, an Italian sailor, led a voyage on behalf of Spain. He sailed west from Europe intending to reach Asia but instead landed in the Americas. This was land that Europeans had not known existed before. Columbus thought at first that he had reached Asia, or the Indies. He misnamed the natives he met Indians and claimed the land for Spain. The king and queen agreed to let him lead another voyage. This one was an expedition to form colonies, or controlled lands, that Spain would rule.

In 1500, a Portuguese explorer landed in Brazil and claimed that land for his country. In 1501, another Italian sailor on behalf of Spain, Amerigo Vespucci, explored the eastern coast of South America. He said that these lands were not Asia but a new world. Soon after, a mapmaker showed the lands as a separate continent. He named them America after Vespucci.

Other voyages gave Europeans more knowledge about the world. One explorer reached the west coast of Central America and first saw the Pacific Ocean. Another, Ferdinand Magellan, led a bold expedition from Spain that sailed completely around the world. Magellan himself died about halfway around. However, a few members of his crew survived. They returned to Spain after sailing for almost three years.

Spanish conquistadors, or conquerors, also began to explore the lands of the Americas. There they found great riches. In 1519, Hernando Cortés came to Mexico and defeated the powerful Aztec Empire. The Spanish had the advantage of rifles and cannons. They also had the aid of several native groups who were angry over harsh Aztec

rule. In addition, the Aztec were seriously weakened by new diseases brought to the Americas with the Spanish. Native peoples had no resistance to measles, mumps, and smallpox, which killed them by the hundreds of thousands.

About 15 years later, another Spanish force, led by Francisco Pizarro, conquered the mighty Inca Empire of South America. Once again, the Spanish gained access to huge amounts of gold and silver. By the mid-1500s, Spain had formed an American empire that stretched from modern-day Mexico to Peru. After 1540, the Spanish looked north of Mexico and explored the future United States. However, one large area of the Americas—Brazil—remained outside the control of Spain. Brazil was the possession of Portugal. Colonists there built huge farms called plantations to grow sugar, which was in demand in Europe.

The Spanish had a pattern of living among the people they conquered. Because few Spanish settlers in the Americas were women, Spanish men had children with native women. These children and their descendants formed a large mestizo population, people with mixed Spanish and Native American blood. The Spanish also formed large farms and mines that used natives as slave labor. Many landowners treated the native workers harshly. Some Spanish priests criticized this treatment. In 1542, the Spanish stopped making slaves of native peoples. They soon, however, would bring enslaved Africans to the Americas to meet labor demands.

❷ European Nations Settle North America

KEY IDEA *Several European nations fought for control of North America, and England eventually emerged victorious.*

In the early 1500s, the French began to explore North America. Jacques Cartier came across and named the St. Lawrence River. He then followed it inward to reach the site of modern Montreal. In 1608, Samuel de Champlain sailed as far as modern Quebec. In the next 100 years, the French explored and claimed the area around the Great Lakes and the Mississippi River all the way to its mouth at the Gulf of Mexico. The area became known as New France. The main activity in this colony was trade in beaver fur.

The English also began to colonize North America. The first permanent settlement came at Jamestown, in modern Virginia, in 1607. The colony struggled at first. Many settlers died from disease, hunger, or war with the native peoples. Soon farmers began to grow tobacco to meet the high demand for it in Europe.

In the 1620s and 1630s, other groups from England began to settle in modern Massachusetts. These settlers were deeply religious people who did not agree with the practices of the Church of England. They wanted to purify the church and were called Puritans. They hoped to build a model community dedicated to God. They succeeded over time in part because many families settled there.

Meanwhile, the Dutch also started a new colony. They settled in the location of modern New York City and called it New Netherland. Like the French, they engaged in the fur trade and set up trading posts along the Hudson River. The colony did not grow very large, but it did attract people from other European countries. New Netherland became known as a home to people of many different cultures. Europeans also took possession of many islands of the Caribbean. There they built tobacco and sugar plantations that used enslaved Africans as workers.

The European powers began to fight for control of North America. First, the English forced the Dutch to give up their colony. New Amsterdam was renamed New York. The English also planted other colonies along the Atlantic coast, from Maine to Georgia. These colonists came in conflict with the French settlers in Canada on many occasions. The final fight started in 1754 and was called the French and Indian War. When it ended in 1763, France was forced to give up all its land in North America to Britain.

The native peoples responded to these events in many different ways. Many worked closely with the French and Dutch, joining in the fur trade and benefiting from it. Those who lived near the English, though, had stormier relations with colonists. More than just trade, the English were interested in

acquiring land for settlers' living and farming. This was land that Native Americans would not be able to use for hunting or growing their own food. This conflict erupted into war several times. Natives, though, could not overcome the settlers' guns and cannons. As in Spanish lands, the native peoples suffered even more from disease. Thousands upon thousands of natives died from European illnesses, making it impossible for them to resist the growth of the colonies.

❸ The Atlantic Slave Trade

KEY IDEA *To meet their growing labor needs, Europeans enslaved millions of Africans in forced labor in the Americas.*

Slavery has a long history in Africa and in the world. For most of that history in Africa, though, no large numbers of people were enslaved. That changed in the 600s, when Muslim traders started to take large numbers of slaves. Between 650 and 1600, Muslims took about 17 million Africans to North Africa and Southwest Asia. Most did have certain rights. The European slave trade that began in the 1500s was larger. Also, the enslaved Africans were treated far more harshly.

In the Americas, when the natives began dying from disease, the Europeans brought in Africans, for three reasons. Africans had resistance to European diseases, so they would not get sick and die. Also, many Africans knew about farming so they would be accustomed to the work involved. Third, Africans were strangers to the Americas and would know no places to hide from slavery. From 1500 to 1870, when the slave trade in the Americas finally ended, about 9.5 million Africans had been imported as slaves.

The Spanish first began the practice of bringing Africans to the Americas. However, the Portuguese—looking for workers for sugar plantations in Brazil—increased the demand for slaves. During the 1600s, Brazil received more than 40 percent of all the Africans sent to the Americas. Other European colonies also brought slaves to work on tobacco, sugar, and coffee plantations. About 400,000 slaves were brought to the English colonies in North America. Their population increased over time, though, to number about 2 million in 1830.

Many African rulers joined in the slave trade. They moved inland to capture people and brought them to the coast to sell to European traders.

This trade was part of a triangular trade that linked Europe, Africa, and the Americas. European ships brought manufactured goods to Africa, trading them for people. They carried Africans across the Atlantic to the Americas, where they were sold into slavery. The traders then bought sugar, coffee, and tobacco, which they carried back to Europe. Another triangle involved ships sailing from the northern English colonies in North America. They carried rum to Africa, people to the West Indies, and sugar and molasses back to the colonies to make more rum.

The part of the voyage that brought people to the Americas was called the middle passage. It was harsh and cruel. People were crammed into ships, beaten, and given little food. Many died, and many others simply jumped overboard trying to escape. About 20 percent of the people on these ships died.

Life on the plantations was harsh as well. People were sold to the highest bidder and then worked from dawn to dusk in the fields of the plantations. They were given little food and lived in small huts. Africans kept alive their traditional music and beliefs to try to maintain their spirits. Sometimes they arose in rebellion. From North America to Brazil, from 1522 to the 1800s, there were small-scale slave revolts.

❹ The Columbian Exchange and Global Trade

KEY IDEA *The colonization of the Americas introduced new and different items into the Eastern and Western hemispheres.*

There was constant movement of people from Europe and Africa to the Americas. This large-scale mixing of people and culture was called the Columbian Exchange. Important foods such as corn and potatoes were taken from the Americas, where they originated, to Europe, Africa, and Asia.

Some foods moved from the Old World to the New. Bananas, black-eyed peas, and yams were taken from Africa to the Americas. Cattle, pigs, and horses had never been seen in the Americas until the Europeans brought them. Of course, deadly illnesses also moved to the Americas. They killed a large portion of the Native American population.

The settling of the Americas and the growth of trade led to a new set of business practices still followed today. One was the rise of an economic system called capitalism. It is based on private owner-ship of property and the right of a business to earn a profit. Another new business idea was the joint-stock company. With this, many investors pooled their money to start a business and share in the profits. European governments began to follow an idea called mercantilism. In this theory, a country's power depended on its wealth. Getting more gold and silver increased its wealth, as would selling more goods than it bought. Colonies played an important role because they provided goods that could be sold in trade.

With the American colonies, European society saw changes. Merchants grew wealthy and powerful, and towns and cities grew larger. Still, most people lived in the countryside, farmed for a living, and were poor.

Review

1. ***Drawing Conclusions*** What single factor was most devastating for the native peoples of the Americas and what effect did it have?

Analyzing Causes and Recognizing Effects

2. How did settlement patterns in the Spanish colonies lead to a mixing of Spanish and native cultures?

3. Why did the French and Dutch have better relations with the native peoples than the English?

4. ***Comparing and Contrasting*** Compare and contrast the Muslim slave trade in Africa with the European slave trade that began in the 1500s.

5. ***Summarizing*** What was exchanged in the Columbian Exchange?

Answer Key

Chapter 4

SUMMARY

The Atlantic World, 1492–1800

Responses will vary but should include points similar to the following:

1. European diseases, to which the native peoples had no resistance; the diseases killed millions of Native Americans and weakened their ability to resist European power.

2. The Spanish had a pattern of living among the people they conquered. So when few Spanish women came to the Americas to settle, Spanish men had children with native women, mixing the cultures.

3. The French and Dutch wanted mostly to trade with the native peoples. The English, though, wanted land for farming and to expand their settlers' populations.

4. The Muslim slave trade was smaller and less harsh. Enslaved Africans worked in Muslim lands and kept some rights. The European slave trade was nearly twice as large, the passage to the New World was harsh and cruel, and work on the plantations was difficult.

5. Food—such as corn and potatoes—moved from the New World to the Old. Bananas, yams, and black-eyed peas as well as large animals such as cattle and horses moved from the Old World to the New. Diseases came from the Old World to the New, which had a devastating effect on the population of Native Americans.

CHAPTER **5** Summary

CHAPTERS IN BRIEF *Absolute Monarchs in Europe, 1500–1800*

CHAPTER OVERVIEW *Spain lost territory and money. The Netherlands split from Spain and grew rich from trade. For a time, France was Europe's most powerful country, where King Louis XIV ruled with total control. Austria's queen resisted a Prussian land grab. Peter the Great modernized Russia. England's Parliament struggled with different kings and became the greatest power in the country.*

❶ Spain's Empire and European Absolutism

KEY IDEA During a time of religious and economic instability, Philip II ruled Spain with a strong hand.

Charles V ruled the Holy Roman Empire and various other European countries. In 1556, he retired from the throne and split his holdings. His brother Ferdinand received Austria and the Holy Roman Empire. His son, Philip II, got Spain and its colonies.

Philip expanded his holdings by taking Portugal and gaining its global territories. When he tried to invade England in 1588, though, he failed. The defeat made Spain weaker. However, Spain still seemed strong because of its wealth—gold and silver—that flowed in from the colonies in the Americas.

This wealth led to some serious problems, however. The prices of goods constantly rose. Also, unfair taxes hit the poor, keeping them from building up any wealth of their own. As prices rose, Spaniards bought more goods from other lands. The silver from the colonies, then, began to flow to Spain's enemies.

In the middle of these troubles, Spain lost land. Seven provinces of the Spanish Netherlands rose in protest against high taxes. Also, they were Protestant and Spain was strongly Catholic. In 1579, these seven provinces declared their independence from Spain.

In the new Dutch republic, each province had a leader elected by the people. The Dutch also practiced religious tolerance, letting people worship as they wished. Dutch merchants established a trading empire. They had the largest fleet of merchant ships in the world and were the most important bankers in Europe.

Though he lost possessions, Philip held tight control over Spain. He and others who ruled in the same way were called absolute monarchs. They believed in holding all power. The Church's power had weakened, which helped make this possible. Some absolute rulers ended conflict within their countries by increasing their power. That is what happened in France.

❷ The Reign of Louis XIV

KEY IDEA After a century of wars and riots, Louis XIV, the most powerful monarch of his time, ruled France.

France was torn by eight religious wars between Catholics and Protestants from 1562 to 1598. In 1589, a Protestant prince, Henry of Navarre, became King Henry IV. He changed religions in 1593, becoming a Catholic to please the majority of his people. In 1598, he issued an order called the Edict of Nantes. It gave Huguenots—French Protestants—the right to live in peace and have their own churches in some cities.

Henry rebuilt the French economy and brought peace to the land. He was followed by his son, a weak king. However, that son had a very capable chief minister, Cardinal Richelieu. He ruled the land for him and increased the power of the crown.

The cardinal ordered that Huguenots could not build walls for their cities. He also said nobles had to destroy their castles. As a result, Protestants and nobles could not hide within walls to defy the king's power. Richelieu used people from the middle class—not nobles—to work in his government. That also cut nobles' power.

French thinkers had reacted to the religious wars with horror. They developed a new attitude—skepticism. Nothing could be known for certain, they argued. Doubting old ideas was the first step to learning the truth, they said.

In 1643, Louis XIV, age four, became king. Cardinal Mazarin ruled for him until Louis was 22. Louis became a powerful ruler, with total control.

Louis determined never to let nobles challenge him.

He froze the nobles out of his government. He gave more power to government officials and made sure that they answered only to him. He also worked hard to increase the wealth of France. His chief minister of finance, Jean Baptiste Colbert, tried to build French industry. Colbert aimed to convince French people to buy French-made goods and not those from other countries. He urged people to settle in the new French colony in Canada. The fur trade there brought wealth to France.

Louis enjoyed a life of luxury at his court. He built a huge and beautiful palace at Versailles near Paris. He also made sure that nobles had to depend on his favor in order to advance in society.

Louis made France the most powerful nation in Europe. France had more people and a larger army than any other country. However, Louis made some mistakes that later proved costly. After winning some wars against neighboring countries, he became bolder and tried to seize more land. Other nations joined together to stop France by the late 1680s. The high cost of these wars combined with poor harvests to produce problems at home in France.

The final war fought in Louis's time lasted from 1700 to 1714. In this War of the Spanish Succession, France and Spain attempted to set up united thrones. The rest of Europe felt threatened and joined in war against them. Both France and Spain were forced to give up some of their American and European colonies to England, the new rising power.

❸ Central European Monarchs Clash

KEY IDEA *After a period of turmoil, absolute monarchs ruled Austria and the German state of Prussia.*

Germany had suffered from religious wars that ended in 1555. Rulers of each state agreed that they would decide whether their lands would be Catholic or Protestant. Over the next decades, though, the two sides had tense relations. In 1618, a new war broke out and lasted for 30 terrible years.

In the first half of the war, Catholic forces led by Ferdinand, the Holy Roman Emperor, won. However, Germany suffered, because he allowed his large army to loot towns. Then the Protestant king of Sweden won several battles against him. In the last years of the war, France helped the Protestants. Although France was a Catholic nation,

Richelieu feared growing Hapsburg family power.

The Thirty Years' War ended in 1648 with the Peace of Westphalia. It had been a disaster for Germany. About 4 million people had died, and the economy was in ruins. It took Germany two centuries to recover. The peace weakened the power of Austria and Spain and made France stronger. Because of this war, each nation of Europe was seen as having an equal right to negotiate with all the others.

While strong states arose in western Europe, none emerged in central Europe. The economies there were less developed than in the West. Most people were still peasants. This region had not built an economy based in towns. Nobles enjoyed great power, which kept the power of rulers in check. Still, two important powers arose.

The Hapsburg family ruled Austria, Hungary, and Bohemia in an empire that linked many different peoples. Maria Theresa, Queen of Austria, managed to increase her power and cut that of the nobles. She was opposed by the kings of Prussia, a new state in northern Germany. Those kings built a strong state with much power given to the large, well-trained army. In 1740, Frederick the Great of Prussia invaded one of Maria Theresa's lands. The queen fought hard to keep the territory, but lost. Still, in fighting this War of the Austrian Succession, she managed to keep the rest of her empire intact. The two sides fought again beginning in 1756. In this Seven Years' War, Austria abandoned Britain, its old ally, for France and Russia. Prussia joined with Britain. The Prussians and British won. In that victory, Britain gained complete control over France's colonies in North America and India.

❹ Absolute Rulers of Russia

KEY IDEA *Peter the Great made many changes in Russia to try to make it more like western Europe.*

Ivan III had made Moscow the center of a new Russian state with a central government. His son continued that work. His grandson, Ivan IV—called Ivan the Terrible—began as a successful ruler. He added lands to Russia and gave the country a code of laws. After his wife died, however, he ruled harshly. He used secret police to hunt down opponents and kill them. Ivan even killed his own oldest son. A few years after he died, Russian nobles met to name a new ruler. They chose Michael Romanov, the grandnephew of Ivan IV's wife. He began a dynasty that ruled Russia for about 300 years.

The Romanovs restored order to Russia. In the late 1600s, Peter I—called Peter the Great—began an intense program of trying to modernize Russia. Peter admired the nations of western Europe. He traveled in Europe to learn about new technology and ways of working. He returned to Russia determined to make his country more advanced. His first steps were to increase the powers of the czar, or ruler, so he could force people to make the changes he wanted. He put the Russian Orthodox Church under his own control. He cut the power of nobles. He built up the army and made it better trained.

He took several steps to make Russia more western. He brought potatoes as a new food, began Russia's first newspaper, gave more social status to women, and told the nobles to adopt Western clothes. He promoted education and built a grand new capital city, St. Petersburg, on the shores of the Baltic Sea.

⑤ Parliament Limits the English Monarchy

KEY IDEA *Absolute monarchs in England were overthrown, and Parliament gained power.*

When Queen Elizabeth I died, her cousin James, king of Scotland, became king of England. James fought with Parliament over money. His religious policies also angered the Puritans in Parliament. They wanted to reform the English church to rid it of Catholic practices. James was unwilling to make these changes.

His son, Charles I, continued the tension between king and Parliament. Parliament forced him to sign a Petition of Right in 1628. By signing, Charles allowed that the king was answerable to Parliament. Then he dissolved the Parliament and tried to raise money without it—going directly against the Petition of Right.

Other actions of Charles had caused Scotland to threaten to invade England. To meet the danger, Charles needed some money, and to raise taxes he needed Parliament. When Charles called a new Parliament, it quickly passed laws to limit his power. Charles responded by trying to arrest its leaders. Soon England was plunged into a civil war: Charles and his Royalists against the supporters of Parliament, many of whom were Puritans.

The English Civil War lasted from 1642 to 1649. Under the leadership of Oliver Cromwell, the forces of the Puritans won. They tried and executed Charles for treason—the first time a king had ever been executed in public. Cromwell became a military dictator, ruling until 1658. He crushed a rebellion in Ireland and tried to reform society at home. Soon after his death, though, the government collapsed. The new Parliament asked Charles's older son to restore the monarchy. Charles II began to rule in 1660.

Charles II's reign was a period of calm after turmoil. After his death in 1685, James II became king. His pro-Catholic policies angered and worried the English, who feared that he would restore Catholicism. Finally, in 1688, seven members of Parliament contacted James's older daughter, Mary, and her husband, William of Orange, prince of the Netherlands—both Protestants. They wanted them to replace James II on the throne. The event was called the Glorious Revolution, a bloodless revolution that forced James to flee to France. William and Mary agreed, swearing to rule according to the laws made by Parliament. They agreed to accept the Bill of Rights, which guaranteed English people certain rights. From then on, no king or queen could rule England without the consent of Parliament.

Review

1. *Analyzing Causes and Recognizing Effects* Why did Spain weaken in power?
2. *Summarizing* How did Richelieu and Louis XIV increase the power of the French king?
3. *Analyzing Causes and Recognizing Effects* How did the Thirty Years' War affect Germany?
4. *Clarifying* What did Peter the Great do to modernize Russia?
5. *Drawing Conclusions* How did England develop away from an absolute monarchy?

Answer Key
Chapter 5
SUMMARY

Absolute Monarchs in Europe, 1500–1800

Responses will vary but should include points similar to the following:

1. Spain weakened in part because it lost the effort to invade England and because it lost the Spanish Netherlands. Also, the economy was weakened by several factors, including the constant rising of prices, overtaxing of the poor, and loss of silver to other nations.

2. Richelieu and Louis XIV broke the power of nobles, reduced the power of the French Protestants, and hired people from the middle-class—not nobles—for the government and then kept in close communication with those officials.

3. The Thirty Years' War devastated Germany, killing about 4 million people and weakening the economy. Germany would take about 200 years to recover.

4. Peter first increased the power of the czar by gaining control over the Russian Orthodox Church and by cutting the power of nobles. He built up the army and made it better trained, brought potatoes as a new food, began Russia's first newspaper, gave more social status to women, told the nobles to adopt Western clothes, and promoted education.

5. The Petition of Right of 1628 put some limits on the ruler's power. With the English Civil War and the execution of Charles I, Parliament showed that it had more power than did the king. That was also established firmly by the Glorious Revolution of 1688 and by the Bill of Rights.

CHAPTER 6

Summary

CHAPTERS IN BRIEF *Enlightenment and Revolution, 1550–1789*

CHAPTER OVERVIEW *Starting in the 1500s, European thinkers overturned old ideas about the physical world with a new approach to science. Thinkers of the Enlightenment hoped to use reason to make a better society in which people were free. Enlightenment ideas spread throughout Europe. They had a profound effect in North America, forming the basis of the new government of the United States.*

❶ The Scientific Revolution

KEY IDEA *In the mid-1500s, scientists began to question accepted beliefs and make new theories based on experimentation.*

During the Middle Ages, few scholars questioned ideas that had always been accepted. Europeans based ideas about the physical world on what ancient Greeks and Romans believed or what was said in the Bible. Therefore, people still thought that the earth was the center of the universe. To them, the sun, moon, other planets, and stars moved around it.

In the mid-1500s, however, attitudes changed. Scholars now started a scientific revolution drawn from a spirit of curiosity. One factor was the new focus on careful observation. Another was the willingness to question old beliefs. European explorations were a third factor. When they reached new lands, Europeans saw new plants and animals never seen by ancient writers. These discoveries led to the opening of new courses of study in universities.

The first challenge came in astronomy. In the early 1500s, Nicolaus Copernicus studied the stars and planets for many years. He concluded that the earth, like the other planets, revolved around the sun, and the moon revolved around the earth. Fearing attack, he did not publish his findings until just before his death. In the early 1600s, Johannes Kepler used mathematics to confirm Copernicus's basic idea.

An Italian scientist—Galileo Galilei—made several discoveries that undercut ancient ideas. He made one of the first telescopes and used it to study the planets. He found that Jupiter had moons, the sun had spots, and Earth's moon was rough. These statements went against church teaching, and Galileo was forced to deny their truth. Still, his ideas spread.

Interest in science led to a new approach, the scientific method. With this method, scientists ask a question based on something they have seen in the physical world. They form a hypothesis, or an attempt to answer the question. Then they test the hypothesis by making experiments or checking other facts. Finally, they change the hypothesis if needed. The English writer Francis Bacon helped foster this new approach to knowledge by telling scientists they should base their ideas on what they can see and test in the world. The French mathematician René Descartes also had great influence. His thinking was based on logic and mathematics.

In the mid-1600s, the English scientist Isaac Newton described the law of gravity. Using mathematics, Newton showed that the same force ruled the motion of planets and the action of bodies on the earth.

Scientists made new tools to study the world around them. One invented a microscope to study creatures too small for the naked eye to see. Others invented tools for understanding weather.

Doctors also made advances. One made drawings that showed the different parts of the human body. Another learned how the heart pumped blood through the body. In the late 1700s, Edward Jenner first used the process called vaccination to prevent disease. By giving a person the germs from a cattle disease called cowpox, he helped that person avoid getting the more serious human disease of smallpox. Scientists made advances in chemistry as well. One challenged the old idea that things were made of only four elements—earth, air, fire, and water. He and other scientists were able to separate oxygen from air.

❷ The Enlightenment in Europe

KEY IDEA *A revolution in intellectual activity changed Europeans' view of government and society.*

New ways of thinking arose in other areas. In the intellectual movement called the

Enlightenment, thinkers tried to apply reason and scientific method to laws that shaped human actions. They hoped to build a society founded on ideas of the Scientific Revolution.

Two English writers were important to this movement. Thomas Hobbes wrote that without a government, there would be a war of "every man against every man." As a result, Hobbes said, people formed a social contract—an agreement—in which they gave up their rights so they could secure order and safety. The best government, he said, is that of a strong king who can force people to obey. John Locke believed that all people have the rights to life, liberty, and property. The purpose of government is to protect those rights. When it fails to do so, he said, people have a right to overthrow the government.

A group of French thinkers had wide influence. They had five main beliefs: (1) thinkers can find the truth by using reason; (2) what is natural is good and reasonable, and human actions are shaped by natural laws; (3) acting according to nature can bring happiness; (4) by taking a scientific view, people and society can make progress and advance to a better life; and (5) by using reason, people can gain freedom.

Three French thinkers had great influence. Voltaire wrote against intolerance and criticized the laws and customs of France. The Baron de Montesquieu made a long study of laws and governments. He thought government power should be separated into different branches. Each should be able to check the other branches to prevent them from abusing their power. Jean Jacques Rousseau wrote strongly in favor of human freedom. He wanted a society in which all people were equal. The Italian Cesare Beccaria wrote about crime and justice. Trials should be fair, he said, and punishments should be made to fit the crime.

Many Enlightenment thinkers held traditional views about women's place in society. They urged equal rights for all men but ignored the fact that women did not enjoy such rights. Some women protested this unfairness. "If all men are born free," wrote one, "how is it that all women are born slaves?"

Enlightenment ideas had strong influence on the American and French Revolutions, which came at the end of the 1700s. They had three other effects. They helped spread the idea of progress. By using reason, people thought, it is possible to make society better. These ideas also helped make Western society more secular—that is, more worldly and less spiritual. Finally, Enlightenment ideas promoted the notion that the individual person was important.

❸ The Enlightenment Spreads

KEY IDEA *Enlightenment ideas spread through the Western world, and influenced the arts and government.*

In the 1700s, Paris was the cultural center of Europe. People came there from other countries in Europe and from the Americas to hear the new ideas of the Enlightenment. Writers and artists gathered in the homes of wealthy people to talk about ideas. A woman named Marie-Thérèse Geoffrin became famous for hosting these discussions. She also supplied the money for one of the major projects of the Enlightenment. With her funds, Denis Diderot and other thinkers wrote and published a huge set of books called the *Encyclopedia*. Their aim was to gather together all that was known about the world. The French government and officials in the Catholic Church did not like many of the ideas that were published in the *Encyclopedia*. They banned the books at first, but later they revoked the ban.

Through the meetings in homes and works like the *Encyclopedia*, the ideas of the Enlightenment spread throughout Europe. The ideas also spread to the growing middle class. This group of people was becoming wealthy but had less social status than nobles and had very little political power. Ideas about equality sounded good to them.

Art moved in new directions, inspired by the Enlightenment ideas of order and reason. Artists and architects worked to show balance and elegance. Composers wrote music of great appeal for their creative richness. In this period, the novel became a popular form of literature. This new form told lengthy stories with many twists of plot that explored the thoughts and feelings of characters.

Some Enlightenment thinkers believed that the best form of government was a monarchy. In it, a ruler respected the rights of people. They tried to influence rulers to rule fairly. Rulers followed these ideas in part but were unwilling to give up much power. Frederick the Great made changes in Prussia. He gave his people religious freedom, improved schooling, and reformed the justice system. However, he did nothing to end serfdom, which made peasants slaves to the wealthy landowners. Joseph II of Austria did end serfdom. Once he died, though, the nobles who owned the land were able to undo his reform.

Catherine the Great of Russia was another of the rulers influenced by Enlightenment ideas. She tried to reform Russia's laws but met resistance. She hoped to end serfdom, but a bloody peasants' revolt convinced her to change her mind. Instead, she gave the nobles even more power over serfs. Catherine did manage to gain new land for Russia. Russia, Prussia, and Austria agreed to divide Poland among themselves. As a result, Poland disappeared as a separate nation for almost 150 years.

❹ The American Revolution

KEY IDEA *Enlightenment ideas help spur the American colonies to create a new nation.*

The British colonies in North America grew in population and wealth during the 1700s. The 13 colonies also enjoyed a kind of self-government. People in the colonies began to see themselves less and less as British subjects. Still, Parliament passed laws that governed the colonies. One set of laws banned trade with any nation other than Britain.

The high cost of the French and Indian War, which ended in 1763, led Parliament to pass laws that put taxes on the colonists. The colonists became very angry. They had never paid taxes directly to the British government before. They said that the taxes violated their rights. Since Parliament had no members from the colonies, they said, Parliament had no right to pass tax laws that affected the colonies. They met the first tax, passed in 1765, with a boycott of British goods. Their refusal to buy British products was very effective and forced Parliament to repeal the law.

Over the next decade, colonists and Britain grew further apart. Some colonists wanted to push the colonies to independence. They took actions that caused Britain to act harshly. These harsh responses, in turn, angered some moderate colonists. Eventually, the conflict led to shooting. Representatives of the colonists met in a congress and formed an army. In July of 1776, they announced that they were independent of Britain. They issued a Declaration of Independence that was based on the ideas of the Enlightenment.

From 1775 to 1781, the colonists and Britain fought a war in North America. The colonists had a poorly equipped army and the British were powerful. However, in the end, they won their independence. The British people grew tired of the cost of the war and pushed Parliament to agree to a peace. The Americans were also helped greatly by aid from France. In 1783, the two sides signed a treaty in which Britain recognized the independent United States.

The 13 states formed a new government that was very weak. It struggled for a few years, but states held all the power and the central government had little. In 1787, many leaders met again and wrote a new framework of government.

The Constitution of the United States drew on many Enlightenment ideas. From Montesquieu, it put in effect the separation of powers into three branches of government. Each branch was able to prevent other branches from abusing their power. From Locke, it put power in the hands of the people. From Voltaire, it protected the rights of people to free speech and freedom of religion. From Beccaria, it set up a fair system of justice. Many of these rights were ensured in a set of additions to the Constitution called the Bill of Rights. Approval of these additions helped win approval of the Constitution as a whole.

Review

1. *Contrasting* Contrast how people in the Middle Ages and people in the scientific revolution looked at the physical world.
2. *Determining Main Ideas* How is the scientific revolution connected to the Enlightenment?
3. *Drawing Conclusions* What were three major ideas of the Enlightenment?
4. *Analyzing Causes and Recognizing Effects* What factors led to the spread of the Enlightenment?
5. *Analyzing Issues* How did the government of the United States reflect Enlightenment ideas?

Answer Key
Chapter 6
SUMMARY

Enlightenment and Revolution, 1550–1789

Responses will vary but should include points similar to the following:

1. In the Middle Ages, scholars based their ideas on what had been written by ancient writers and what was in the Bible. In the scientific revolution, scholars based their ideas on what they had observed firsthand and a willingness to question old beliefs.

2. The Enlightenment thought that advances in science were due to the use of reason. They hoped to apply reason to social and political issues, rather than the description of nature.

3. Enlightenment ideas included the rights to life, liberty, and property; that reason can gain people freedom; that government power should be separate and balanced; that trials should be fair; and that all men should have equal rights.

4. The discussions held in fashionable French homes and publication of the *Encyclopedia* helped spread the ideas of the Enlightenment.

5. From Montesquieu, the Constitution of the United States put in effect the separation of powers into three branches of government. Each branch was able to prevent other branches from abusing their power. From Locke, it put power in the hands of the people. From Voltaire, it protected the rights of people to free speech and freedom of religion. From Beccaria, it set up a fair system of justice. Many of these rights were ensured in a set of additions to the Constitution called the Bill of Rights.

CHAPTER
7
Summary

CHAPTERS IN BRIEF *The French Revolution and Napoleon, 1789–1815*

CHAPTER OVERVIEW France's lower classes revolted against the king. Thousands died. Napoleon took control of France and created an empire. After his defeat, European leaders restored the rule of monarchs to the continent.

❶ The French Revolution Begins

KEY IDEA *Economic and social inequalities in the Old Regime helped cause the French Revolution.*

In the 1700s, France was the leading country of Europe. It was the center of the new ideas of the Enlightenment. However, beneath the surface there were major problems causing unrest. Soon the nation would be torn by a violent revolution.

One problem was that people were not treated equally in French society. The French were divided into three classes, or estates. The First Estate consisted of the Roman Catholic clergy. The Second Estate was made up of rich nobles. Only about two percent of the people belonged to these two estates. Yet they owned 20 percent of the land and paid little or no taxes. They had easy lives.

Everybody else belonged to the Third Estate. This huge group included three types of people:

• the bourgeoisie—mostly well-off merchants and skilled workers who lacked the status of nobles
• city workers—cooks, servants, and others who were poorly paid and often out of work
• peasants—farm workers, making up more than 80 percent of the French people

Members of the Third Estate were angry. They had few rights. They paid up to half of their income in taxes, while the rich paid almost none.

Three factors led to revolution. First, the Enlightenment spread the idea that everyone should be equal. The powerless people in the Third Estate liked that. Second, the French economy was failing. High taxes kept profits low, and food supplies were short. The government owed money. Third, King Louis XVI was a weak, unconcerned leader. His wife, Marie Antoinette, was a big spender and was disliked.

In the 1780s, deeply in debt, France needed money. Louis tried to tax the nobles. Instead, they forced the king to call a meeting of delegates of the three estates to decide tax issues. The meeting began in May 1789 with arguments over how to count votes. In the past, each estate had cast one vote. The top two estates always voted together and got their way. Now the Third Estate delegates wanted to change the system. The Third Estate had as many delegates as the other two estates combined. They wanted each delegate to have a vote. The king and the other estates did not agree to the plan.

The Third Estate then broke with the others and met separately. In June 1789, its delegates voted to rename themselves the National Assembly. They claimed to represent all the people. This was the beginning of representative government for France.

Louis tried to make peace. He ordered the clergy and nobles to join the National Assembly. However, trouble erupted. Rumors flew that Swiss soldiers paid by Louis were going to attack French citizens. On July 14, an angry crowd captured the Bastille, a Paris prison. The mob wanted to get gunpowder for their weapons in order to defend the city.

A wave of violence called the Great Fear swept the country. Peasants broke into and burned nobles' houses. They tore up documents that had forced them to pay fees to the nobles. Late in 1789, a mob of women marched from Paris to the king's palace at Versailles. They were angry about high bread prices and demanded that the king move to Paris. They hoped he would end hunger in the city. The king and queen left Versailles, never to return.

❷ Revolution Brings Reform and Terror

KEY IDEA *The revolutionary government of France made reforms but also used terror and violence to retain power.*

In August 1789, the National Assembly took steps to change France. One new law ended all the special privileges that members of the First and Second Estates had enjoyed. Another law gave all French men equal rights. Though women did not get these rights, it was a bold step. Other laws cut the power of the Catholic Church. The government took over church lands, hoping to sell them and raise money.

The new laws about the church divided people who had backed the Revolution. Catholic peasants remained loyal to the church. They were angry that the church would be part of the state. Thereafter, many of them opposed the Revolution's reforms.

For months the assembly worked on plans for a new government. During this time, Louis was fearful for his safety in France. One night he and his family tried to escape the country. They were caught, brought back to Paris, and lived under guard. After this, the king and queen were even less popular.

In the fall of 1791, the assembly drew up a new constitution that gave the king very little power. The assembly then handed over its power to a new assembly, the Legislative Assembly. After the new assembly began to meet, however, it divided into opposing groups. Some wanted an end to revolutionary changes. Others wanted even more radical changes.

At the same time, France faced serious trouble on its borders. Kings in other countries feared that the French Revolution would spread to their lands. They wanted to use force to restore control of France to Louis XVI. Soon France found itself at war—a war it quickly began to lose. Foreign soldiers were coming near to Paris. Many people thought that the king and queen were ready to help the enemy. Angry French citizens imprisoned them. Many nobles were killed in other mob action.

The government took strong steps to meet the danger from foreign troops. It took away the king's powers. In 1792, the National Convention—another new government—was formed. It declared Louis a common citizen and then put him to death. It also ordered thousands of French people into the army.

Soon one man, Maximilien Robespierre, began to lead France. He made many changes. He ordered the death of many people who did not agree with him. His rule, which began in 1793, was called the Reign of Terror. It ended in July 1794, when Robespierre himself was put to death.

France got a new, but less revolutionary, plan of government. Tired of the killing and unrest, the French people wanted a return to order.

❸ Napoleon Forges an Empire

KEY IDEA *Napoleon Bonaparte, a military genius, seized power in France and made himself emperor.*

Napoleon Bonaparte became the master of France. In 1795, he led soldiers against French royalists who were attacking the National Convention. For this, he was hailed as the savior of the French republic. Later he invaded Italy to end the threat from Austrian troops located there.

By 1799, the unsettled French government had lost the people's support. In a bold move, Napoleon used troops to seize control of the government. He then wielded complete power over the country. Other nations feared his power and attacked France again. Napoleon led his armies into battle. In 1802, the three nations fighting him agreed to a peace. Napoleon went back to solve problems at home.

He made several changes that were meant to build on the Revolution's good ideas:

1. He made tax collection more fair and orderly. As a result, the government could count on a steady supply of money.
2. He removed dishonest government workers.
3. He started new public schools for ordinary citizens.
4. He gave the church back some of its power.
5. He wrote a new set of laws that gave all French citizens the same rights. However, the new laws took away many individual rights won during the Revolution. For example, they limited free speech and restored slavery in French colonies.

Napoleon had hoped to make his empire larger in both Europe and the New World. In 1801, he had sent soldiers to retake the island of present-day Haiti. During a civil war, slaves on the island had seized power. But Napoleon had to give up on his plan. Too many of his soldiers died in battle or from disease. Napoleon eventually abandoned his New World plans. In 1803, he sold the largest part of France's North American land—the huge Louisiana Territory—to the United States.

Stopped in the Americas, Napoleon moved to add to his power in Europe. In 1804, he made himself emperor of France. He quickly captured country after country. Other nations joined against him. However, after Napoleon won a major battle in Austria in 1805, almost all of his European enemies agreed to a peace treaty. Napoleon's only loss during this time was to the British navy off the southwest coast of Spain. This loss prevented him from invading and conquering Britain. That failure would be costly.

❹ Napoleon's Empire Collapses

KEY IDEA *Napoleon's conquests aroused nationalistic feelings across Europe and contributed to his downfall.*

Napoleon loved power. He took steps to make his empire larger. However, these steps led to mistakes that brought about his downfall.

Napoleon's first mistake was caused by his desire to crush Britain. He wanted to hurt the British economy. So in 1806 he tried stopping all trade between Britain and the lands he controlled. The effort failed, for some Europeans secretly brought in British goods. At the same time, the British put their own blockade around Europe. Because their navy was so strong, it worked very well. Soon the French economy, along with others, began to grow weak.

Napoleon's second mistake was to make his brother king of Spain in 1808. The Spanish people were loyal to their own king. With help from Britain, they fought back against Napoleon for five years. Napoleon lost 300,000 troops.

Napoleon's third mistake was perhaps his worst. In 1812, he tried to conquer Russia, far to the east. He entered Russia with more than 400,000 soldiers. He got as far as Moscow, which was deserted and on fire. His soldiers found no food or supplies there. Winter was coming, and Napoleon ordered them to head back to France. As the soldiers marched west, bitter cold, hunger, and attacks by Russian troops killed thousands. Thousands more deserted. By the time the army exited Russian territory, only 10,000 of its men were able to fight.

Other leaders saw that Napoleon was weaker now, and they moved to attack. He was defeated in Germany in 1813. In 1814, Napoleon gave up his throne and was sent away. Nevertheless, in March 1815, he boldly returned to France. He took power and raised another army. By June, though, Napoleon had lost his final battle near a Belgian town called Waterloo. This time he was sent to a far-off island in the southern Atlantic Ocean. He died there in 1821.

❺ The Congress of Vienna

KEY IDEA *After exiling Napoleon, European leaders at the Congress of Vienna tried to restore order and reestablish peace.*

After Napoleon's first defeat, in 1814, leaders of many nations met for months. They tried to draw up a peace plan for Europe that would last many years. They called the meeting the Congress of Vienna. The key person there was the foreign minister of Austria, Klemens von Metternich. He shaped the peace conditions that were accepted.

Metternich insisted on three goals. First, he wanted to make sure that the French would not attack another country again. Second, he wanted a balance of power in which no one nation was too strong. Third, he wanted to put kings back in charge of the countries from which they had been removed. The leaders agreed with Metternich's ideas. An age of European peace began.

Across Europe, kings and princes reclaimed their thrones. Most of them were conservatives and did not encourage individual liberties. They did not want any calls for equal rights. However, many people still believed in the ideals of the French Revolution. They thought that all people should be equal and share in power. Later they would fight for these rights again.

People in the Americas also felt the desire for freedom. Spanish colonies in the Americas revolted against the restored Spanish king. Many nations won independence from Spain. National feeling grew in many places in Europe, too. Soon people in areas such as Italy, Germany, and Greece would rebel and form new countries. The French Revolution had changed the politics of Europe and beyond.

Review

1. *Analyzing Causes* What factors led to the French Revolution?
2. *Following Chronological Order* Trace the fate of Louis XVI during the Revolution.
3. *Summarizing* What did Napoleon do to restore order in France?
4. *Making Inferences* Why did Napoleon's empire collapse?
5. *Determining Main Ideas* What were the goals of the Congress of Vienna?

Answer Key
Chapter 7
SUMMARY

The French Revolution and Napoleon, 1789–1815

Responses will vary but should include points similar to the following:

1. The members of the Third Estate, nearly 98 percent of France's population, were angry about their high taxes and lack of privileges. Enlightenment thinkers spread ideas about basic rights and equality. The French economy was failing, with low profits, shortages of food, and government debt. The king was weak and the queen was unpopular.

2. Louis and his family attempted to flee France but were captured. The National Assembly took away most of his powers. Other countries hoped to restore Louis to the French throne. He was imprisoned when it was thought he would help those countries. Finally, his powers were removed entirely, and he was executed as a common person.

3. He made taxes more equal and their collection more orderly; he removed dishonest government workers; he set up new public schools for ordinary citizens; he restored some church power; and he made new laws that gave citizens equal rights, though some rights were restricted.

4. He made three mistakes: trying to blockade Britain, which reacted by putting a stronger blockade on Europe; putting his brother on the Spanish throne, which caused the Spanish people to fight back; and invading Russia, where his army was nearly destroyed by brutal winter weather.

5. The congress weakened France so that it could not attack another country; created a balance of power in which no nation would be too strong; and restored monarchs to their throne.

CHAPTER **8** Summary

CHAPTERS IN BRIEF *Nationalist Revolutions Sweep the West, 1789–1900*

CHAPTER OVERVIEW *Spurred by the French Revolution, Latin American colonies won independence. In Europe, liberals and radicals pushed for change but conservatives resisted. Nationalism spread throughout Europe, and Germany and Italy formed as nations. Artistic and intellectual movements emphasized nature and feelings, true life, and "impressions" of a subject or moment.*

❶ Latin American Peoples Win Independence

KEY IDEA Spurred by discontent and Enlightenment ideas, peoples in Latin America fought colonial rule.

In the early 1800s, colonial peoples throughout Latin America followed the example of the French Revolution. In the name of freedom and equality, they fought for their independence.

In Latin America, society was divided into six classes of people. *Peninsulares*—those born in Spain—were at the top. Next came creoles, or Spaniards who had been born in Latin America. Below them were mestizos, with mixed European and Indian ancestry. Next were mulattos, with mixed European and African ancestry, and Africans. At the bottom were Indians.

The first movement for independence was the French colony of Saint Domingue, on the island of Hispaniola. Almost all of the people who lived in the colony were slaves of African origin. In 1791, about 100,000 of them rose in revolt. Toussaint L'Ouverture became the leader. By 1801, he had moved to the eastern part of the island and freed the slaves there. In 1804, the former colony declared its independence as Haiti.

Meanwhile in other parts of Latin America, creoles felt that they were unfairly treated by the government and the *peninsulares*. This bad feeling boiled over when Napoleon overthrew the king of Spain and named his own brother as king. Creoles in Latin America had no loyalty to the new king and revolted. However, even after the old king was restored, they did not give up their fight for freedom.

Two leaders pushed much of South America to independence. Simón Bolívar was a writer, fighter, and political thinker. He survived defeats and exile to win independence for Venezuela in 1821. José de San Martín helped win independence for Argentina in 1816 and Chile in 1818. Bolívar led their combined armies to a great victory in 1824

that gave independence to all the former Spanish colonies.

Turmoil continued in the region. Local leaders disagreed and split the new countries up into smaller units. In 1830, the territory of Gran Colombia divided into Colombia, Ecuador, and Venezuela.

In Mexico, mestizos and Indians led the fight for independence. The struggle began in 1810 when Miguel Hidalgo, a village priest, called for a revolt against Spanish rule. Creoles united with the Spanish government to put down this revolt by the lower classes, whom they feared. Fighting continued until 1815, when the creoles won. In 1820, a new government took charge in Spain. Fearing that they would lose their rights this time, the creoles now united with the rebels and fought for independence. In 1821, Spain accepted Mexico's independence. In 1823, the region of Central America separated itself from Mexico. In 1841, the United Provinces of Central America split into five republics.

In Brazil, independence took a different turn. When Napoleon's armies entered Portugal in 1807, the royal family escaped to Brazil, its largest colony. For the next 14 years, it was the center of the Portuguese empire. By the time Napoleon was defeated, the people of Brazil wanted their independence. In 1822, 8,000 creoles signed a paper asking the son of Portugal's king to rule an independent Brazil. He agreed, and Brazil became free that year through a bloodless revolt.

❷ Europe Faces Revolutions

KEY IDEA Liberal and nationalist uprisings challenged the old conservative order of Europe.

In the first half of the 1800s, three forces struggled for power within the countries of Europe. Conservatives supported the kings who had ruled these lands for many centuries. These were nobles and other people who owned large amounts of property. Liberals wanted to give more power to elected legislatures. They were typically middle-class merchants and business people. They wanted to limit voting rights to people who were educated and owned property. Radicals wanted the end of rule by kings and full voting rights for all people, even the poor.

At the same time, another movement arose in Europe—nationalism. This was the belief that a person's loyalty should go not to the country's ruler but to the nation itself. Nationalists thought that many factors linked people to one another. First was nationality, or a common ethnic ancestry. Shared language, culture, history, and religion were also seen as ties that connected people. People sharing these traits were thought to have a right to a land they could call their own. Groups with their own government were called nation-states. Leaders began to see that this feeling could be a powerful force for uniting a people. The French Revolution was a prime example of this.

The first people to win self-rule during this period were the Greeks. For centuries, Greece had been part of the Ottoman Empire. In 1821, Greeks revolted against this Turkish rule. Rulers in Europe did not like the idea of revolts, but the Greek cause was popular. Other nations gave aid to the Greeks, helping to defeat the Ottomans' forces in 1827. The Greeks won their independence by 1830.

Other revolts broke out. In 1830, the Belgians declared their independence from rule by the Dutch. Nationalists began a long struggle to unify all of Italy, which had been broken into many different states. Poles revolted against Russian rule. Conservatives managed to put down these rebellions. However, new ones broke out again in 1848 among Hungarians and Czechs. Once again, they were put down forcefully.

Events differed in France. Riots in 1830 forced the king to flee and put a new king in his place. A new revolt broke out in 1848 that overthrew the king and established a republic. However, the radicals who had won this victory began arguing over how much France should be changed. Some wanted only political changes. Others wanted social and economic changes that would help the poor. When these forces fought in the streets, the French gave up on the radical program. They introduced a new government, with a legislature and a strong president. The new president was Louis-Napoleon, Napoleon Bonaparte's nephew. He later named

himself emperor of France. He built railroads and promoted the growth of France's industry. The economy revived and more people had jobs.

Russia in the early 1800s had yet to build an industrial economy. The biggest problem was that serfdom still existed there. Peasants were bound to the nobles whose land they worked. Russia's rulers did not wish to free the serfs, though. They feared they would lose the support of the nobles. In the 1850s, the Russian army lost a war to take over part of the Ottoman Empire. The new ruler of Russia, Alexander II, decided that Russia's lack of a modern economy caused the defeat. He decided to begin many reforms.

The first, in 1861, was to free the serfs. Though it seemed bold, Alexander's move went only part way. Nobles kept half their land and were paid for the half that went to the peasants. The former serfs were not given the land. They had to pay for it, and this debt kept them still tied to the land. The czar's efforts to make changes ended short when he was assassinated in 1881. Alexander III, his successor, brought back tight control over the country and moved to make the economy more industrial.

❸ Nationalism Case Study: Italy and Germany

KEY IDEA *The force of nationalism contributed to the formation of two new nations and a new political order in Europe.*

Nationalism can be a force uniting people who are divided from others like themselves. The case studies on Germany and Italy will show this. However, nationalism can also cause the break-up of a state. This may occur when a group resists being part of a state. The Greeks in the Ottoman empire are an example. Finally, nationalism can pull different groups together to build a nation-state. The United States is a good example of this.

In the late 1800s, feelings of nationalism threatened to break apart three aging empires. The Austrian Empire was forced to split in two parts, Austria and Hungary. However, nationalist feeling continued to plague these rulers for 40 years and the kingdoms later broke up into several smaller states. In Russia, harsh rule and a policy of forcing other peoples to adopt Russian ways helped produce a revolution in 1917 that overthrew the czar. The Ottoman Empire, like the other two, broke apart around the time of World War I.

Italians used national feeling to build a nation, not destroy an empire. Large parts of Italy were ruled by the kings of Austria and Spain. Nationalists tried to unite the nation in 1848, but the revolt was beaten down. Hopes rested with the Italian king of the state of Piedmont-Sardinia. His chief minister, Count Cavour, worked to expand the king's control over other areas of the north. Meanwhile, Giuseppi Garibaldi led an army of patriots that won control of southern areas. He put those areas under control of the king. In 1866, the area around Venice was added to the king's control. Four years later, the king completed the uniting of Italy.

Germany had also been divided into many different states for many centuries. Since 1815, 39 states had joined in a league called the German Confederation. Prussia and Austria-Hungary controlled this group. Over time, Prussia rose to become more powerful. Leading this move was prime minister Otto von Bismarck. He joined with Austria to gain control of new lands. He then quickly turned against Austria, defeating it in war to gain even more territory. Other German states formed a new confederation that Prussia alone controlled. Bismarck's next step was to win the loyalty of the remaining German areas in the south. He purposefully angered a weak France so that it would declare war on Prussia. When the Prussian army won, Bismarck reached his goal. The war with France had given the southern German states a nationalistic feeling. They joined the other states in naming the king of Prussia as head of united Germany.

As a result of these events, the balance of power in Europe had changed. Germany and Britain were the strongest powers, followed by France. Austria, Russia, and Italy were all even weaker.

❹ Revolutions in the Arts

KEY IDEA *Artistic and intellectual movements both reflected and fueled changes in Europe in the 1800s.*

In the early 1800s, the Enlightenment was replaced by another movement, called romanticism. This movement in art and ideas showed great interest in nature and in the thoughts and feelings of the individual person. Gone was the idea that reason and order were good things. Romantic thinkers valued feeling, not reason, and nature, not society. Romantic thinkers held idealized views of the past as simpler, better times. They valued the common people. As a result, they enjoyed folk sto-

ries, songs, and traditions. They also supported calls for democracy. However, not all romantic artists and thinkers supported these ideas.

Romantic writers had different themes. French writer Victor Hugo—who wrote *The Hunchback of Notre Dame*—told stories of the poor individual who fights against an unfair society. English poet William Wordsworth celebrated the beauty of nature. Novels such as Mary Shelley's *Frankenstein* were horror tales about good and evil.

Romanticism was important in music as well. Composers wrote music that tried to appeal to the hearts and souls of listeners. The German Ludwig van Beethoven was the foremost of these composers.

In the middle 1800s, however, the grim realities of industrial life made the dreams of romanticism seem silly. A new movement arose—realism. Artists and writers tried to show life as it really was. They used their art to protest social conditions that they thought were unfair. French writer Emile Zola's books revealed harsh working conditions for the poor, which led to new laws aimed at helping those people. In England, Charles Dickens wrote many novels that showed how poor people suffered in the new industrial economy.

A new device, the camera, was developed in this period. Photographers could use it to capture a real moment on film. In the 1860s, Parisian painters reacted against the realistic style. This new art style—impressionism—used light and shimmering colors to produce an "impression" of a subject or moment. Composers created moods with their music. They used combinations of musical instruments and tone patterns to create mental pictures. Things like the sight of the sea or a warm day were favorites of the composers.

Review

1. *Making Inferences* How did the divisions of Mexican society affect the movement to independence?
Drawing Conclusions
2. Explain how the freeing of Russia's serfs in 1861 was an example of both liberal and conservative thought.
3. Give one example each of how nationalism was a unifying and a destructive force.
4. *Determining Main Ideas* How did artistic ideas change in the 1800s?

Answer Key
Chapter 8
SUMMARY

Nationalist Revolutions Sweep the West, 1789–1900

Responses will vary but should include points similar to the following:

1. The divisions in society may have prevented Mexican independence from happening earlier. Creoles did not at first join the revolt because they were afraid of the lower classes.

2. Freeing serfs from being bound to the nobles for whom they worked was a liberal thought. However, making serfs pay for the land was a conservative thought. It created a debt that kept them tied to the land.

3. Nationalism was a destructive force in Austria, where it forced the empire to divide into the kingdoms of Austria and Hungary and later resulted in the complete breakup of those kingdoms. Nationalism was a unifying force in Italy.

4. In the early 1800s, the main artistic movement was romanticism, which valued feeling, nature, and the past. In the middle 1800s, the main movement was realism, which showed the world as it really was. Finally, impressionism caught an "impression" of a subject or a moment.

CHAPTER
9
Summary

CHAPTERS IN BRIEF *The Industrial Revolution,*
1700–1900

CHAPTER OVERVIEW *Britain fueled an Industrial Revolution, which changed society. Workers benefited eventually, but at first they suffered bad working and living conditions. Other nations followed Britain's example and industrialized. Thinkers reacted to these changes by developing new views of society. Reformers pushed for changes to make society better.*

❶ The Beginnings of Industrialization

KEY IDEA *The Industrial Revolution started in Great Britain and soon spread elsewhere.*

In the early 1700s, large landowners in Britain bought much of the land that had been owned by poorer farmers. They introduced new ways of farming. One technique was to use a seed drill. This machine planted seeds in well-spaced rows. Before this, seeds were scattered by hand over the ground. As a result, more seeds sprouted. Another technique was to rotate crops annually. Those who raised livestock used new methods to increase the size of their animals. As a result of these improvements, farm output increased. More food was available, and people enjoyed healthier diets. The population of Britain grew. The agricultural revolution helped produce the Industrial Revolution.

The Industrial Revolution refers to the greatly increased output of machine-made goods that began in Great Britain in the mid–1700s.

For several reasons, Britain was the first country to have an economy based on industry. It had 1) coal and water to power machines, 2) iron ore to make machines and tools, 3) rivers to move people and goods, and 4) good harbors for shipping goods to other lands. Britain also had a system of banks that could fund new businesses. Finally, the British government was stable, which gave the country a positive attitude.

The Industrial Revolution began in the textile industry. Several new inventions helped businesses produce cloth and clothing more quickly. Business owners built huge buildings—factories—that housed large machines powered by water.

The invention of the steam engine in 1705 brought in a new source of power. The steam engine used fire to heat water and produce steam, which was used to drive the engine. Eventually steam-driven machines were used to run factories.

At the same time, improvements were being made in transportation. An American invented the first steam-driven boat. This allowed people to send goods more quickly over rivers and canals. The British also built better roads that included layers of stone and rock to prevent wagons from being stuck in the mud.

Starting in the 1820s, steam fueled a new burst of industrial growth. At that time, a British engineer set up the world's first railroad line. It used a steam-driven locomotive. Soon, railroads were being built all over Britain. The railroad boom helped business owners move their goods to market more quickly. The boom in railroad building created thousands of new jobs in several different industries. The railroad had a deep effect on British society. For instance, people who lived in the country moved to cities.

❷ Industrialization Case Study: Manchester

KEY IDEA *The factory system changed the way people lived and worked, ibringing both benefits and problems.*

The change to an industrial economy brought many benefits to British people. They used coal to heat their homes, ate better food, and wore better clothing. Many people also suffered, however. Industrialization caused many changes.

One change was a rise in the proportion of people who lived in cities. For centuries, most people in Europe had lived in the country. Now more and more lived in cities. The number of cities with more than 100,000 people doubled between 1800 and 1850. Because they grew quickly, cities were not ideal places to live. People could not find good housing, schools, or police protection. The cities were filthy with garbage, and sickness swept through slum areas. The average life span of a person living in a city was 17 years—compared to 38 years in the countryside.

Working conditions were harsh as well. The average worker spent 14 hours a day on the job, 6 days a week. Factories were dark, and the powerful machines were dangerous. Many workers were killed or seriously injured in accidents. Some rioted against the poor living and working conditions.

Some people improved their lives in the new economy. The middle class—made up of skilled workers, professionals, business people, and wealthy farmers—did well. They enjoyed comfortable lives in pleasant homes. This class began to grow in size, and some people in it grew wealthier than the nobles who had dominated society for many centuries. Still, nobles looked down on the people who gained their wealth from business. They, in turn, looked down on the poor workers.

Overall, the Industrial Revolution had many good effects. It increased the amount of goods and services a nation could produce and added to its wealth. It created jobs for workers and over time helped them live better lives. It produced better diets, better housing, and cheaper, better clothing. Many of these benefits were far in the future, however.

The English city of Manchester showed how industrialization changed society. Rapid growth made the city crowded and filthy. The factory owners risked their money and worked long hours to make their businesses grow. In return, they enjoyed huge profits and built huge houses. The workers also worked long hours, but had few benefits.

Many workers were children, some only six years old. Not until 1819 did the British government put limits on using children as workers. With so much industry in one place, Manchester suffered in another way. Coal smoke and cloth dyes polluted the air and water. Yet, Manchester also created many jobs, a variety of consumer goods, and great wealth.

❸ Industrialization Spreads

KEY IDEA *The industrialization that began in Great Britain spread to other parts of the world.*

Other countries followed the example of Britain and began to change their economies to an industrial base. The United States was one of the first. Like Britain, it had water power, sources of coal and iron, and a ready supply of workers. The United States also benefited from conflict with Britain. During the War of 1812, Britain stopped shipping goods to the United States. As a result, American industries had a chance to supply the goods that Americans wanted.

The switch to an industrial economy began in the United States in the textile industry. In 1789, based on memory and a partial design, a British worker brought the secret of Britain's textile machines to North America. He built a machine to spin thread. In 1813, a group of Massachusetts investors built a complex of factories that made cloth. Just a few years later they built an even larger complex in the town of Lowell. Thousands of workers, mostly young girls, came to these towns to work in the factories.

In the United States, industry grew first in the Northeast. In the last decades of the 1800s, a rapid burst of industrial growth took place that was more widespread. This boom was fueled by large supplies of coal, oil, and iron. Helping, too, was the appearance of a number of new inventions, including the electric light. As in Britain, railroad building was also a big part of this industrial growth.

Businesses needed huge sums of money to take on big projects. To raise money, companies sold shares of ownership, called stock. All those who held stock were part owners of the company. This form of organizing a business is called a corporation.

Industrial growth spread to Europe as well. Belgium was the first to adopt British ways. It was rich in iron and coal and had good waterways. It had the resources needed.

Germany was politically divided until the late 1800s. As a result, it could not develop a wide industrial economy. However, west-central Germany was rich in coal and did become a leading industrial site.

Across Europe, small areas began to change to the new industries. Industrial growth did not occur in France until after 1830. It was helped by the government's construction of a large network of railroads. Some countries—such as Austria-Hungary and Spain—had problems that stopped them from building new industries.

The Industrial Revolution changed the world. Countries that had adopted an industrial economy enjoyed more wealth and power than those that had not. The countries of Europe soon began to take advantage of lands in Africa and Asia. They used these lands as sources of raw materials needed for their factories. They saw the people only as markets for the goods they made. They took control of these lands, a practice called imperialism.

The Industrial Revolution changed life forever in the countries that industrialized. Problems

caused by industrialization led to movements for
social reform.

➍ Reforming the Industrial World

KEY IDEA *The Industrial Revolution led to economic,
social, and political reforms.*

The new industrial economy led to new ways
of thinking about society. Some economists
thought that the government should leave business
owners alone. Their view was called laissez-faire,
from a French phrase meaning "let people do as
they please." Adam Smith argued that putting no
limits on business or on trade would help a nation's
economy grow the most. He and other economists
supported a system called capitalism. In a capitalist
economy, people invest their money in businesses
to make a profit. Over time, society as a whole
would benefit, said Smith and the others. These
people warned the government not to make laws
trying to protect workers. Such laws would upset the
workings of the economy, they said.

Other thinkers challenged these ideas. One
group was called the Utilitarians. They thought that
an idea or practice was good only as it proved use-
ful. They thought it was unfair that workers should
work so hard for such little pay and live in such
poor conditions. They thought the government
should do away with great differences in wealth
among people.

Some thinkers went farther and urged that businesses should be owned by society as a whole, not
by individuals. Then a few people would not grow
wealthy at the expense of many. Instead, all would
enjoy the benefits of increased production. This
view—called socialism—grew out of a belief in
progress and a concern for justice and fairness.

A German thinker named Karl Marx wrote
about a radical form of socialism called Marxism.
He said that factory owners and workers were
bound to oppose one another in the struggle for
power. Over time, he said, the capitalist system
would destroy itself. The great mass of workers
would rebel against the wealthy few. Marx wrote
The Communist Manifesto in which he described
communism, a form of complete socialism in which
all production is owned by the people. Private
property would not exist. In the early 1900s, these
ideas would inspire revolution.

While thinkers discussed these different ideas,
workers took action to try to improve their lives.
Many formed into unions that tried to bargain with
business owners for better pay and better working
conditions. When business owners resisted these
efforts, the workers went on strike, or refused to
work. The struggle to win the right to form unions
was long and hard for workers in Britain and the
United States. Still, by the late 1800s, workers in
both countries had made some progress.

The British Parliament and reformers in the
United States also took steps to try to fix some of
the worst features of industrialism. Britain passed
laws that put limits on how much women and children could work. Groups in the United States
pushed for similar laws.

Another major reform movement of the 1800s
was the drive to abolish slavery. The British
Parliament took the first step by ending the slave
trade in 1807. It abolished slavery completely in
1833. Slavery was finally ended in the United States
in 1865, after the Civil War. Spain ended slavery in
Puerto Rico in 1873 and in Cuba in 1886. Brazil
became the last country to ban slavery, which it did
in 1888.

Women were active in these and other reform
movements. As they fought for the end of slavery,
many women launched an effort to win equal rights
for women. The movement for equality began in
the United States in 1848. In 1888, women from
around the world formed a group dedicated to this
cause.

Reformers took on other projects as well. Some
pushed for—and won—improved education.
Others hoped to improve conditions in prisons.

Review

1. *Analyzing Causes and Recognizing Effects*
   Why did the Industrial Revolution begin in
   Britain?
Determining Main Ideas
2. What was the impact of the railroad?
3. What reforms were popular in the 1800s?
4. *Analyzing Causes and Recognizing Effects*
   What effects did industrialization have on
   society?
5. *Developing Historical Perspective* How did
   industrialization spread in the United States?

Answer Key
Chapter 9
SUMMARY

The Industrial Revolution, 1700–1900

Responses will vary but should include points similar to the following:

1. Britain had some advantages: it had resources such as coal and water to power machines, iron ore to make tools and machines, rivers to move people and goods, and good harbors for shipping goods to other lands. Britain also had a system of banks that could fund new businesses. Finally, the British government was stable, and people were optimistic.

2. The railroad boom helped business owners move their goods to market more quickly. The boom in railroad building created thousands of new jobs in several different industries. People who lived in the country moved to cities.

3. Reformers pushed for limits on how much women and children could work, the end of slavery, equal rights for women, and improved education and prisons.

4. The population of cities grew, although cities were crowded, dirty, and unhealthy places. Economies grew, and people could enjoy a better standard of living. Diet and education improved. Many of these changes took a long time to reach the masses of workers, however.

5. After industrialization came to the United States, it was limited mostly to the Northeast. However, toward the end of the 1800s, it spread across the country. That spread was promoted by several inventions, the building of railroads, and the growth of cities.

CHAPTERS IN BRIEF *An Age of Democracy and Progress, 1815–1914*

CHAPTER OVERVIEW In Britain, reforms gave all men the right to vote. A republic was proclaimed in France, but political conflict continued. Some British colonies won the right to govern themselves, but the struggle for that right was not easy in Ireland. The United States fought a civil war that finally put an end to slavery. New inventions and scientific advances made life more healthful and enjoyable.

❶ Democratic Reform and Activism

KEY IDEA Spurred by the demands of ordinary people, Great Britain and France underwent democratic reforms.

Since the 1600s, Britain's government had been a constitutional monarchy. A king or queen ruled the country, but the elected legislature—Parliament—held the real power. Still, very few people could vote for members of Parliament. Only men who owned property—about six percent of the population—had the right. That changed in the 1800s.

The Reform Bill of 1832 was the first step. Middle-class people across England protested the fact that they could not vote. Worried by revolutions sweeping Europe, Parliament passed the Reform Bill. This law gave the right to vote to many in the middle class. It also gave seats in Parliament to the new industrial cities, which had not had any representatives before. Over time, Parliament made more changes. By 1884, almost all adult males in Britain could vote. Parliament also made votes take place by secret ballot. Another law gave pay to members of Parliament, which in effect opened that body to people who were not wealthy.

By 1890, a number of countries with industrial economies had given all men the right to vote. None, however, gave women that right. During the 1800s, women in the United States and Britain peacefully campaigned for the vote. Beginning in 1903, a group called the Women's Social and Political Union began a stronger campaign for women's suffrage in Britain. They held rallies and parades. They also broke up the speeches of government officials and sometimes set fire to buildings. When the leaders were arrested, they went on hunger strikes to gain publicity for their cause. It was not until after World War I, however, that women won the right to vote in both Great Britain and the United States.

The road to democracy in France was more rocky. After France's defeat at the hands of Prussia in 1870, France went through a series of crises. Finally a new government—the Third Republic—was formed. It lasted over 60 years, but France remained divided.

In the 1890s, French society was divided over the case of an army officer, Alfred Dreyfus, who was accused of being a traitor. The charge was false and was made largely because Dreyfus was a Jew. However, many believed the charge, and he was found guilty. A few years later, new evidence showed that he had been framed. Dreyfus was later declared innocent.

The affair revealed that many in Europe hated Jews. In Eastern Europe, the situation was very bad. The Russian government even allowed organized attacks on Jewish villages. From the 1880s on, many Jews fled to the United States.

❷ Self-Rule for British Colonies

KEY IDEA Britain allowed self-rule in Canada, Australia, and New Zealand but delayed independence for Ireland.

Britain had colonies all around the world. Three of them were settled by colonists from Europe who built societies strongly shaped by British culture. Canada, Australia, and New Zealand developed industrial economies. They reached a point where they hoped to have their own governments.

The white settlers of Canada were split into two groups. Britain had won Canada from France back in 1763. However, some French-speaking Catholics still lived in the colony. The other group was English-speaking and mostly Protestant. The two groups did not get along. In 1791, Britain split the colony into two provinces, each with its own government. The French-speaking people grew angry at British rule.

After a series of rebellions, the British Parliament put the two sections back together under one government. Other, smaller colonies were added to create the Dominion of Canada. Canadians had the right to make all laws concerning their own affairs. Parliament kept the right to make decisions about relations with other countries. By 1871, Canada stretched all the way to the Pacific Ocean.

New Zealand and Australia first became part of the British Empire around 1770. The first settlers sent to Australia were convicted criminals. Once they had spent the required amount of time, they won their freedom and had the right to buy land. In the 1800s, other settlers arrived, many to join in the growing sheep industry. The settlement of New Zealand went more slowly because the British government recognized that the native people—the Maori—had rights to the land. By the 1840s, though, the number of settlers was growing.

During the 1850s, these two countries became self-governing. However, they stayed in the British Empire and in the early 1900s became dominions. Australia was the first country to use secret ballots in voting for representatives. New Zealand—in 1893—was the first country to give women the right to vote. The native peoples of Australia and New Zealand enjoyed few of these rights, though. Like Native Americans, they suffered the spread of European settlement.

Irish self-rule took longer to achieve. Ireland bitterly opposed English rule from its start in the 1100s. Conflict also separated the Catholic Irish and the small group of English Protestants. When Ireland was made part of Britain in 1801, the Irish won representation in Parliament. A leader used that position to win back some rights for Irish Catholics.

In the 1840s, the Irish suffered a terrible famine. A disease destroyed the potatoes on which the Irish depended, causing many to starve. About 1 million died and another 1.5 million left for the United States and other countries. Meanwhile, the British forced the Irish to pay their rents. Many lost their land, and resentment against England grew even stronger.

In the late 1800s, some Irish pushed for complete independence. Most argued for home rule—the right to govern internal affairs. The British government opposed this move. They were afraid that the Catholic majority would harshly treat the Protestants in the north. In 1914, Parliament finally gave home rule to the southern part of Ireland. When World War I delayed its enactment, Irish nationalists rebelled. Finally, Britain split Ireland in two. Northern Ireland remained part of Britain. The southern part became independent. Many people still seek independence for all of Ireland.

❸ War and Expansion in the United States

KEY IDEA *The United States expanded across North America and fought a bloody civil war.*

The United States had troubles of its own. In the early 1800s, the nation grew in size. It bought a huge piece of land from France in the Louisiana Purchase. Many said it was "manifest destiny"—the right of the United States to rule the land from the Atlantic Ocean to the Pacific. As white settlers moved farther and farther west, Native Americans suffered. In the 1830s, many thousands were forced to move from their homes in the eastern states to the present state of Oklahoma. The United States won a war with Mexico in the 1840s and thus gained even more land.

This growth raised serious questions. The southern states used slave labor to grow crops such as cotton. People in the South hoped to extend slavery to the new western lands. Many in the North, however, believed that slavery was wrong and should be ended.

Conflict over slavery eventually led to the Civil War. The southern states seceded, or pulled out of, the Union. When southern forces fired on a Union fort in 1861, war broke out. The fighting lasted four long and bloody years. The North won the war. During the fighting, President Abraham Lincoln declared that slavery was ended in the United States. Later, the Constitution was changed to make this the law of the land and to say that African Americans were citizens.

In the first few years after the war, newly freed African Americans enjoyed equal rights. Later, whites regained control of the governments of the southern states. They passed laws that took away the rights of blacks and treated them unfairly. It would be many years before African Americans could enjoy equality.

The economy of the South was destroyed by the Civil War. Elsewhere, though, the nation saw a surge of industrial growth. Helping achieve this great growth was a sharp rise in immigration from Europe and Asia. By 1914, more than 20 million people had come to the United States.

❹ Nineteenth-Century Progress

KEY IDEA Breakthroughs in science and technology transformed daily life and entertainment.

In the late 1800s, new inventions made major changes in how people lived. Thomas Edison got patents on more than 1,000 inventions. Among them were the electric light bulb and the phonograph. Alexander Graham Bell invented the telephone, and Guglielmo Marconi created the first radio.

There were big changes in transportation too. Though someone else invented the car, Henry Ford made it affordable to ordinary people. He had a factory with an assembly line that allowed him to quickly build cheap cars that cost as little as $300. In 1903, the Wright brothers flew the first motor-powered airplane flight. Soon there was an aircraft industry.

Medicine made advances. Until the mid-1800s, no one knew about germs. French scientist Louis Pasteur discovered that microscopic animals that he called bacteria could live in food. Soon he and others realized that bacteria could cause disease. British surgeon Joseph Lister took steps to kill bacteria, which helped more patients survive. Soon his practices became widespread. Public officials began to clean up plumbing and sewage systems. All these steps helped people lead longer and healthier lives.

English scientist Charles Darwin developed a new theory that was hotly debated. He said that all life on earth, even humans, had developed from simpler forms over millions of years. Many did not accept this idea, which they said went against the Bible.

In the mid-1800s, an Austrian monk named Gregor Mendel did some experiments that showed that parents passed on their traits to offspring. His work formed the basis of the science of genetics. Other scientists made new discoveries in chemistry and physics. They found that all matter is made of tiny particles called atoms. They also were able to identify the differences between different elements.

In the late 1800s, some thinkers began the new social science of psychology, which is the study of the mind. A series of experiments led Russian Ivan Pavlov to argue that people responded to certain situations because of how they were trained. By changing the training, he said, one could change the response. Austrian Sigmund Freud argued that powerful forces in the subconscious mind of a person shaped behavior. These views shocked many. They seemed to overturn the idea that people could use their reason to build better lives.

In earlier times, art, music, and the theater had been of interest only to the wealthy. With the rise of the middle class, culture became available to more people. One reason was that more people could read, which led to more newspapers, magazines, and books.

Another reason was that working people had more time to enjoy art, music, and recreation. People went to music halls to enjoy singing and dancing. In the early 1900s, they began to watch the first silent movies. People also began to enjoy sporting events, both as participants and as spectators.

Review

Comparing and Contrasting

1. Contrast the spread of democracy in Britain with that in France.
2. Compare the development of self-rule in the different colonies of Britain.
3. *Determining Main Ideas* How did the United States change during the 1800s?
4. *Drawing Conclusions* What important inventions were made in the late 1800s and early 1900s? Which one do you think was most important?
5. *Analyzing Causes and Recognizing Effects* How did new medical and scientific discoveries and ideas from the late 1800s change life?

Answer Key
Chapter 10
SUMMARY

An Age of Democracy and Progress, 1815–1914

Responses will vary but should include points similar to the following:

1. In Britain, Parliament extended the right to vote to more people through a peaceful series of changes. In France, the growth of democracy grew out of more conflict.

2. In Canada, self-rule was put in place to try to end the conflict between French-speaking and English-speaking settlers. In Australia and New Zealand, self-rule was granted with little conflict. In Ireland, however, self-rule was only given to part of the island, and that came only after many decades of rebellion.

3. During the 1800s, the United States expanded to the Pacific Ocean, ended slavery, changed to an industrial economy, and saw the arrival of millions of immigrants.

4. In the late 1800s and early 1900s, new inventions included the electric light, the telephone, the radio, the car, and the airplane. Of these, the light was the most important, because it allowed people to live and work at night and helped make streets safer.

5. New medical discoveries revealed that germs can cause disease and allowed doctors and public health officials to take steps to make hospitals and cities healthier. New scientific discoveries revealed new information about genes and atoms. Social scientists developed the new study of psychology, which tried to understand how hidden forces shaped people's behavior.

CHAPTER 11
Summary

CHAPTERS IN BRIEF *The Age of Imperialism, 1850–1914*

CHAPTER OVERVIEW *Several factors led Europeans to claim control of almost all of Africa. Some Africans resisted, but most efforts failed. The Ottoman Empire broke apart, and European powers took some of its lands. The British took control of India, where they modernized the economy to benefit themselves. Europeans gained lands in Southeast Asia, and the United States sought colonies.*

❶ The Scramble for Africa

KEY IDEA *Ignoring the claims of African ethnic groups, kingdoms, and city-states, Europeans established colonial claims.*

In the early 1800s, European nations had just a toehold in Africa, holding only areas along the coast. In the mid-1800s, though, Europeans had renewed interest in Africa. This rose, in part, from a desire to create overseas empires, a movement called imperialism. European nations wanted to control lands that had raw materials they needed for their industrial economies. They also wanted to open up markets for the goods they made. Nationalism fed the drive for empires as well. A nation often felt that gaining colonies was a measure of its greatness. Racism was another reason. Europeans thought that they were better than Africans. Finally, Christian missionaries supported imperialism. They thought that European rule would end the slave trade and help them convert native peoples.

As a result of these factors, the nations of Europe began to seize lands in Africa. Technology helped them succeed. Steamships, railroads, and telegraphs made them able to penetrate deep into Africa and still have contact with the home country. Machine guns gave them a weapon of far greater power than any African peoples possessed. Finally, the drug quinine gave doctors a weapon against malaria, which struck Europeans. They were also helped by the lack of unity among African peoples.

The competition for African land, called the "scramble for Africa" began in the 1880s. The discovery of gold and diamonds in Africa increased European interest in the continent. So that they would not fight over the land, European powers met in Berlin in 1884–85. They agreed that any nation could claim any part of Africa simply by telling the others and by showing that it had control of the area. They then moved quickly to grab land.

By 1914, only Liberia and Ethiopia were independent of European control.

The Europeans began to build plantations where they grew peanuts, palm oil, cocoa, and rubber. They also mined Africa's important minerals. The Congo produced copper and tin. South Africa had gold and diamonds.

In South Africa, three groups struggled over the land. In the early 1800s, the Zulu chief Shaka created a large kingdom. The British seized control of this land in 1887. Meanwhile, the British won control of the Dutch colony on the southern coast. Many thousands of Dutch settlers, called Boers, moved north to escape the British. At the end of the century, the Boers fought a vicious war with the British. The Boers lost, and they joined the British-run Union of South Africa.

❷ Imperialism Case Study: Nigeria

KEY IDEA *Europeans embarked on a new phase of empire-building that affected both Africa and the rest of the world.*

European nations wanted to control more of the life of their conquered peoples. As a result, each colonized region operated under one of these forms:

- colony—governed by a foreign power
- protectorate—allowed its own government but was under the control of a foreign power
- sphere of influence—claimed as the exclusive investment or trading realm of a foreign power
- economic imperialism—controlled by private businesses rather than by a foreign government

The imperialist powers had two main methods of running their colonies. Britain and the United States used indirect control. In this system, local rulers had power over day-to-day matters. There were also councils of native peoples and government officials. These councils were a first step for native peoples to someday govern themselves.

Britain tried to rule Nigeria through indirect control. Because the area was huge and peopled by many different groups, it was difficult for the British to rule directly. They let local chiefs maintain order over their areas and collect taxes. The system did not always work. Chiefs had ruled before in the southeast and southwest of Nigeria. The chiefs resented having their power limited.

France and other European nations used the other method—direct control. Feeling that native peoples could not handle the complex business of running a country, the European power governed. The French also had a policy of assimilation. All institutions were patterned after their counterparts in France. They hoped that the native peoples would learn and adopt French ways.

Some Africans tried to resist imperialism. People in Algeria fought against the French for almost 50 years. In German East Africa, thousands died when they tried to use spiritual power to fight German machine guns. Only in Ethiopia did resistance succeed. There, Emperor Menelik II cleverly played one European country against another. In 1896, he used European weapons to defeat an invading Italian army. With this victory, Ethiopia stayed independent.

Africans did enjoy some benefits from colonial rule. European governments put an end to ethnic conflict. Colonial powers brought African economies fully into the world market and built railroads, dams, and telephone and telegraph lines.

For the most part, though, imperialism caused damage. Traditional African society was destroyed. People were forced out of their homes and made to work under horrible conditions. Finally, the political boundaries that Europeans drew had no relation to ethnic divisions in Africa. These boundaries created problems many decades later when the colonies became independent nations.

❸ Europeans Claim Muslim Lands

KEY IDEA *European nations expand their empires by seizing territories from Muslim states.*

The Ottoman Empire, based in modern Turkey, had lasted for hundreds of years. By the 1800s, it was weak. In 1830, Greece won its independence and Serbia won the right to govern itself. European nations eyed what remained of the empire hungrily.

Russia hoped to win control of the Black Sea so it could ship grain across the Mediterranean Sea. It fought a war with the Ottomans in the 1850s but lost when Britain and France joined against it. Still, the Ottomans later lost almost all of their land in Europe and parts of Africa. By 1914, the empire was much smaller than it had ever been. Muslim leaders, seeing this decline, decided to modernize their countries.

In Egypt, Muhammad Ali broke away from Ottoman control. He put in place reforms to change the army and the economy. He pushed Egypt's farmers to grow cotton, a cash crop in demand in Europe. However, peasants suffered when they were turned away from growing food. His grandson continued to modernize. He joined with the French in building the Suez Canal, which connected the Mediterranean to the Red Sea. When Egypt had money troubles, Britain took control of the canal—and the country.

In Persia, the Russians and the British competed for control with local powers. Russia wanted to win Persia to have access to the Indian Ocean. Britain wanted some land there as a barrier between Russia and its colony in India. In the early 1900s, oil was discovered in Persia. A British company signed an agreement with Persia's ruler to develop these oil fields. Persians rebelled against their ruler—who was corrupt—and the growing influence of Europeans. Then Russia and Britain stepped in and took control of the land.

❹ British Imperialism in India

KEY IDEA *As the Mughal Empire declined, Britain seized almost the whole subcontinent of India.*

In the early 1700s, the Mughal Empire of India fell into decline. By the middle of the century, the British East India Company was becoming the most important power in India. It held huge amounts of land—almost the entire subcontinent.

British law forced India to supply raw materials such as tea, indigo (a dye), coffee, and cotton. The law also forced Indian manufacturing out of business. India became even more important when the East India Company built rail lines that linked growing regions in the interior with ports on the coast.

India enjoyed some gains from British rule. Its rail system was the third largest in the world and helped make the economy more modern. The

British made other improvements, too. They built telephone and telegraph lines, dams, bridges, and canals. They also improved sanitation and public health and built schools. More and more Indians learned to read.

British rule caused problems as well. Many economic benefits flowed out of India to Britain. Indian industry died out because of British trade laws. Many farmers and villages lost their ability to feed themselves because they were made to grow cash crops. Many peoples died when famines struck. British racist attitudes damaged Indian culture.

By the mid-1800s, many Indians felt growing resentment. When Indian soldiers heard rumors that offended their religious feelings, many rebelled. The East India Company needed a year—and British troops—to put it down. The Indians lost because of their own divisions. Muslims and Hindus did not trust each other. After the revolt, the British government took direct control of British India.

Indians tried other ways of resisting British control. Leaders such as Ram Mohun Roy urged changes in traditional Indian practices to make Indian society more modern. He hoped to free India of foreign control with these changes. Indians resented the fact that they were treated unfairly. They formed two groups—the Indian National Congress and the Muslim League. Both began to push the British to make changes. In the early 1900s, they called for self-government.

❺ Imperialism in Southeast Asia

KEY IDEA *Demand for Asian products drove Western imperialists to seek possession of Southeast Asian lands.*

European nations also grabbed land in Southeast Asia and the islands on the edge of the Pacific Ocean. They wanted the area for its resources and because it was close to China. The United States joined this quest for colonies.

European powers found that these lands were good for growing such cash crops as sugar, coffee, cocoa, rubber, and fruit. As trade in these items grew, Europeans moved to take more land. The Dutch ran Indonesia, where their settlers remained at the top of society. The British took the port of Singapore plus Malaysia and Burma (modern Myanmar). Needing workers, the British brought many Chinese to Malaysia. France grabbed Indochina (modern Laos, Cambodia, and Vietnam). They made farmers grow rice for export. Because most of the rice was shipped away, the farmers had less to eat even though they were growing more rice than before. One land—Siam (modern Thailand)—stayed independent. King Mongkut and his son modernized Siam without giving up power.

Colonialism brought some features of modern life to these regions. However, economic changes benefited European-run businesses, not local people. The native peoples did benefit from better schooling, health, and cleanliness. Plantation farming brought millions of people from other areas to Southeast Asia. The mix of cultures and religions did not always go smoothly. Even today, some conflict between groups results from this period.

In the late 1800s, the United States also began to seek colonies. In 1898, as a result of the Spanish-American War, the United States won possession of Puerto Rico, Guam, and the Philippine Islands. Filipino nationalists fought Americans for their freedom, just as they had fought the Spaniards before. The United States defeated the rebels and promised to give the Philippines self-rule later. In the meantime, American businesses took advantage of Filipino workers.

Some American businessmen grew wealthy from sugar plantations in Hawaii. In the 1890s, when Queen Liliuokalani tried to regain control of her country, they overthrew her. They declared a republic and asked the United States to annex—take possession of—Hawaii. In 1898, it became a territory of the United States.

Review

1. **Summarizing** What led to European imperialism, and why did it succeed?
2. **Analyzing Causes and Recognizing Effects** What happened when Africans tried to resist imperialism?
3. **Comparing and Contrasting** Contrast how the British and French ruled their colonies.
4. **Drawing Conclusions** How were the effects of imperialism in Southeast Asia typical of those for other regions?

Answer Key
Chapter 11
SUMMARY

The Age of Imperialism, 1850–1914

Responses will vary but should include points similar to the following:

1. Imperialism arose because Europeans wanted to control lands that had raw materials and provided markets for the goods they made; to promote nationalism; to prove racial superiority; and to make it easier for Christian missionaries to convert native peoples. Imperialism succeeded because of technology (steamships, railroads, telegraphs, and machine guns) and because of the lack of unity among African peoples.

2. When Africans tried to resist imperialism, they were generally defeated, except in the case of the Ethiopian Emperor Menelik II, who had weapons equal to those of the European power he opposed.

3. The British tried to rule their colonies indirectly and hoped that eventually the native peoples could govern themselves. The French ruled their colonies directly and wanted native peoples to adopt French culture.

4. In Southeast Asia as in other regions, steps to modernize the economies generally benefited the European businesses and not the local people. Still, locals did enjoy better schooling, health, and sanitation.

CHAPTER 12

Summary

CHAPTERS IN BRIEF *Transformations Around the Globe, 1800–1914*

CHAPTER OVERVIEW *In China, a weak government could not resist European power. In Japan, a reforming emperor modernized the country and launched imperialist expansion. The Latin American economies fell prey to European businesses, and the United States became the dominant power in the region. A revolution freed Mexico from France, but civil war raged for decades.*

❶ China Resists Outside Influence

KEY IDEA *Western economic pressure forced China to open to foreign trade and influence.*

In the late 1700s, China was self-sufficient. It had a strong farming economy based on growing rice. Other crops, introduced from the Americas, helped to feed its large population. Industry made silk, cotton, and ceramics. Mines produced salt, tin, silver, and iron. China needed nothing from the outside world.

China allowed only limited trade with European powers, and it all had to come through one port. Also, the trade at this port was in China's favor. In other words, the Chinese sold more than they bought. Europeans, especially the British, were eager to find something that the Chinese would want in large quantities. In the early 1800s, they found it—the drug opium, shipped mostly from India. Soon millions of Chinese were addicted to opium, and the Chinese government complained. When the British refused to stop the trade, war broke out. Because British ships had more powerful guns, China lost the war. As a result, in 1842 the British took possession of Hong Kong. Later, the United States and European nations won the right to trade in five ports. The Chinese resented these treaties but could not stop them.

China had internal problems as well. The population had grown quickly. Yet food production had barely increased, so millions starved. The Chinese began to rebel against their government. A leader arose in southern China who hoped to save China. He launched a rebellion that won control of large parts of the south, including the city of Nanjing. The government needed 14 years to put down the Taiping Rebellion. The fighting resulted in the death of millions.

In the late 1800s, European powers and Japan each won a foothold in China—a "sphere of influence." This is a region in which a foreign nation controls trade and investment. The United States opposed these steps. It urged an Open Door Policy, in which all powers had equal access to Chinese markets. While the Europeans agreed, the result had little benefit for China. Though it was not formally carved into colonies, it was clearly dominated by foreign powers.

The Empress Cixi ruled China in fact, even though younger emperors ruled in name. She supported some reforms. She backed the self-strengthening movement, which produced new ships for China. The program was not a complete success, though. In 1898, the young Emperor Guangxu tried to put in place broader reforms. Conservatives didn't like this. The retired Cixi had him arrested and took back control of the government. China had lost a chance to change.

Many Chinese grew increasingly resentful of foreign influence. They formed the Society of Harmonious Fists, known as the Boxers. They wanted to get rid of all Western influence—including any Chinese who had accepted Western culture or the Christian religion. In early 1900, an army of Boxers surrounded Beijing's European section. After many weeks, they were finally driven out by a multinational army of soldiers.

Finally Cixi began to allow major reforms. Change came slowly, though. In 1908, the court said that China would become a constitutional monarchy by 1917. However, unrest would soon return.

❷ Modernization in Japan

KEY IDEA *Japan followed the model of Western powers by expanding its foreign influence.*

From the early 1600s to the mid-1800s, Japan was virtually isolated. It did have relations with China and Korea and had limited contact with Dutch traders. That changed in 1853 when American steamships, with cannons, entered Japanese waters.

The next year, Japan agreed to open up trade to the United States. Soon after, it made similar deals with European nations.

Many Japanese were upset with the shogun, the military dictator, who had agreed to these new treaties. The Emperor Mutsuhito rallied their support and managed to overthrow the shogun. For the first time in centuries, the emperor ruled Japan directly. He reigned for 45 years, from 1867 to 1912, in what is called the Meiji era. The name Meiji, which he chose for his reign, means "enlightened rule."

The emperor was determined to modernize his country. He sent government officials to Europe and the United States. From what they saw, they shaped a new Japan. They modeled the government after the strong central government of Germany. They patterned the army after Germany's and a new navy after Britain's. They adapted the American system of schooling for all children. The emperor also supported changes to Japan's economy. The country built railroads, mined coal, and constructed factories.

These steps had results. In just a few years, Japan's industrial economy equaled almost any in the world. By 1890, it was the strongest military power in Asia. It asked foreigners to give up their special rights in Japan. The countries agreed, and a proud Japan felt equal to them. Now, it wanted to demonstrate its power.

Japan began to expand its influence like the European powers. When China broke an agreement not to send armies into Korea, Japan went to war. It drove China out of Korea and gained Taiwan and some other islands as new colonies. In 1904, Japan and Russia fought a war over China's Manchurian territory. Japan surprised the world by defeating a larger power that was supposed to be stronger.

The next year, Japan attacked Korea, and by 1910 it had won complete control. The Japanese proved to be harsh rulers. They shut down Korean newspapers and changed schools so that only Japanese language and history were taught. They took away land from Korean farmers and gave it to Japanese settlers. They built factories to be run by Japanese only. Koreans were not allowed to start new businesses. Koreans bitterly resented these actions. They began a nationalist movement and protested against Japanese rule.

❸ U.S. Economic Imperialism

KEY IDEA *The United States put increasing economic and political pressure on Latin America in the 1800s.*

In the early 1800s, the new nations of Latin America had serious problems. Most people were poor. They worked on farms for large landowners who took advantage of them. Another problem was political unrest. Local leaders rivaled one another for power. Military dictators, or caudillos, generally held power with the backing of the landowners, because the dictators refused to give power to the mass of poor people. Only people with property could vote. Sometimes reformers did take office and lead their countries. They never lasted long, though. When their reforms upset the power of the wealthy too much, a caudillo would rise and remove them from office.

With Spain no longer ruling the lands, old trade laws were gone. The new countries could now trade with any nation. Britain and the United States became the chief trading partners. Soon businesses in these nations dominated Latin American economies.

The economies of Latin America depended on exporting goods. They shipped goods such as coffee, beef, fruits, and vegetables. Each country focused on producing and exporting one or two goods. The volume of exports rose rapidly during the 1800s. The coming of railroads and steamships helped. The invention of refrigerated cars helped also, allowing producers to increase food exports.

This trade mainly went to benefit other countries, though. Latin America did not develop industries of its own. It had to import manufactured goods, which cost more than what was earned from exports. Also, Latin American countries often borrowed money to expand the facilities used to increase those exports. They had to borrow the money from foreign banks. When they could not repay the loans, lenders took control of the businesses. In this way, much of Latin American business fell into foreign hands.

In the 1890s, the United States began to take a more active role in Latin American affairs. The people of Cuba were fighting for their independence from Spain. American businesses had important interests on the island. Also, Spain had placed Cuban citizens in concentration camps, which outraged many Americans. For these reasons, the United States joined the war. The Spanish quickly gave up, and the United States gained several new territories. After the war, though, the United States put a military government in place in Cuba. This step and others helped promote anger among many Cubans against the United States.

The United States next set its sights on Panama. Ships traveling from the east to the west coast had to go around the southern tip of South America, which took many weeks. Americans hoped to build a canal across Panama. President Roosevelt offered $10 million to Colombia—to which Panama belonged—for the right to build this canal. When Colombia asked for more money, the United States helped the people of Panama revolt for independence. In return, the United States won a ten-mile-wide zone in Panama in which to build a canal. The canal opened in 1914.

In 1904, Roosevelt said that the United States had the right to act as "an international police power" in the western hemisphere. Over the next decades, it acted on that belief many times. When trouble arose in various countries, the United States sent its troops. Sometimes they stayed for many years.

❹ Turmoil and Change in Mexico

KEY IDEA Political, economic, and social inequalities in Mexico triggered a period of revolution and reform.

Antonio López de Santa Anna was a leading figure in the early history of independent Mexico. He fought to win independence from Spain and led in another war when Spain tried to recapture Mexico. He served as president four times, shrewdly changing his positions in order to retain power.

In the 1830s, though, he was unable to prevent people in Texas from winning their freedom from Mexico. In the 1840s, the United States annexed Texas, which angered many Mexicans. When a border dispute broke out, the United States invaded Mexico. Santa Anna led his nation's army and was defeated. Mexico had to surrender huge amounts of land.

Another important leader of the middle 1800s was Benito Juárez. A Zapotec Indian, Juárez wanted to improve conditions for the poor in Mexico. He led a movement called *La Reforma*— the reform—that aimed at breaking the power of the large landowners and giving more schooling to the poor. He and his liberal supporters won control of the government in the late 1850s. The conservatives who opposed them did not give up, however. They plotted with France to retake Mexico. In 1862, Napoleon III of France sent an army that captured the country in 18 months. He named a European noble as emperor. But, Juárez and his followers kept fighting. In 1867, they drove the French from Mexican soil and killed the emperor.

Juárez once again pressed for his reforms. He made some progress but died in office in 1872. Soon after, a new leader emerged. Porfirio Díaz dominated Mexican politics for more than 30 years. Díaz brought order to the country and encouraged economic growth. However, he sharply limited political freedom.

In the early 1900s, calls for reform got louder. Leaders "Pancho" Villa and Emiliano Zapata gathered support with their demand for better lives for the poor. They raised small armies and forced Díaz to step down. Fighting continued, however, for many years as several leaders struggled for power. In the midst of this turmoil, Mexico adopted a new constitution in 1917. It called for breaking up large landholdings and for limits on foreign ownership of business. It promoted the right to strike for workers and promised some rights for women. Conflict continued until a new political party gained control of Mexico in 1929. The Institutional Revolutionary Party (PRI) brought peace and political stability to a troubled land.

Review

1. *Summarizing* Describe China's two major attempts to remain isolated from the outside world.
2. *Recognizing Effects* What was the result of Japan's feelings of pride and strength in the late 1800s?
3. *Evaluating Courses of Action* Through what method did the Japanese modernize during the Meiji era?
4. *Drawing Conclusions* Why did the Latin American nations not benefit from growing trade?
5. *Comparing* What did Juárez, Villa, and Zapata have in common?

Answer Key
Chapter 12
SUMMARY

Transformations Around the Globe, 1800–1914

Responses will vary but should include points similar to the following:

1. In the late 1700s, China allowed only limited trade with Europeans. As a result, China had to fight a war with the British. It lost and was forced to open up the country to foreign trade. In early 1900, a group called the Boxers tried to rid China of Western influences by fighting Europeans in Beijing.

2. A proud Japan wanted the world to see its strength. It turned imperialistic in its own right and attacked China and then warred successfully with Russia.

3. The Japanese borrowed ideas and techniques from Western powers. They selectively took what they wanted from Germany, Britain, and the United States.

4. Latin American nations did not benefit from growing trade because they lacked industry to make manufactured goods. They thus had to buy these goods, but the value of those purchases was more than the value of their exports. Also, they borrowed large amounts of money to finance improvements in facilities. When they could not pay these loans back, foreign investors took control of their industries.

5. They all wanted to improve conditions for the poor in Mexico.

CHAPTER 13 Summary

CHAPTERS IN BRIEF *The Great War, 1914–1918*

CHAPTER OVERVIEW Strong national feelings and strong armies produced competition between European nations and led to war. The system of alliances turned a local conflict into a general European war and then a world war. Horribly brutal, it changed the lives of millions and transformed Russia when it helped cause a revolution.

❶ Marching Toward War

KEY IDEA In Europe, military buildup, nationalistic feelings, and rival alliances led to a continental war.

In the later 1800s, many people in Europe joined groups to promote peace. They met several times between 1843 and 1907 to urge their cause. While this movement for peace was building, so were other developments. These other factors would soon plunge Europe into war.

One of those factors was nationalism—the deep feeling of attachment to one's own nation. This force helped unify the people of a country. It also helped promote competition between countries. By 1900, six nations were rivals for power in Europe. These nations, called the Great Powers, were Germany, Austria-Hungary, Great Britain, Russia, Italy, and France. They competed economically, and they competed for neighboring land.

Imperialism was another force that helped lead to war. France and Germany, each seeking control of parts of Africa, almost came to war twice in the early 1900s. Such competition bred mistrust.

The third factor leading to war was a growing arms race. Each country in Europe—except Great Britain—built a large army. Generals in each country made complex plans to be able to mobilize their armies or rush troops to battle as quickly as possible.

Growing rivalry led the nations to make alliances with one another. Fearing that France would want revenge for its defeat in the Franco-Prussian War, Otto von Bismarck set out to isolate France. In 1879, he formed a Triple Alliance with Austria-Hungary and Italy, and a treaty with Russia. However, when Wilhelm II became kaiser, or emperor, of Germany, he did not want to share power. He forced Bismarck out and followed his own policy. He let the agreement with Russia expire, and Russia quickly allied itself with France. This alliance meant that Germany would have to fight enemies on east and west borders if there were a war with either country. Wilhelm II then moved to make the German navy larger. Britain grew alarmed

and began to build more ships of its own. It made a Triple Entente alliance with France and Russia. The six Great Powers had now formed two camps: Germany, Austria-Hungary, and Italy against Britain, France, and Russia.

Meanwhile, trouble was brewing in the Balkans, in southeastern Europe. The Ottoman Empire, which controlled this area, was breaking apart. Both Austria-Hungary and Russia wanted some of this land. The kingdom of Serbia, which was in this region, wanted to bring other Slavic peoples who lived in the Balkans under its control. In 1908, Austria-Hungary seized Bosnia and Herzegovina. These lands had Slavic peoples, and the Serbs were angered. However, their Russian allies were unwilling to support them, and they backed down.

By 1914, the situation was different. Serbia had gained land in other parts of the region and felt strong. Austria worried that Serbia might interfere with its control of Bosnia and Herzegovina. Amid these tensions, a shot rang out. In June 1914, a Serbian shot and killed the heir to the throne of Austria-Hungary. Austria-Hungary declared war on Serbia, Russia came to Serbia's defense, and soon most of Europe was at war.

❷ Europe Plunges into War

KEY IDEA One European nation after another was drawn into a large and industrialized war that resulted in many casualties.

The system of alliances turned the war between Austria-Hungary and Serbia into a wider war. Russia moved against Austria-Hungary. Figuring that Germany would support Austria-Hungary, Russia moved troops against Germany as well. Germany declared war on Russia. Soon after, it also declared war on France, Russia's ally.

Germany had a plan for winning the war on two fronts. It called for a rapid push through France, a quick defeat of that nation, and a turn to face Russia in the east. To capture France quickly, Germany moved through Belgium, which was a neutral country. Britain was outraged by this and declared war on Germany. France, Britain, and Russia were later joined by Italy, which broke from Germany and Austria-Hungary. They were called the Allies. Bulgaria and the Ottoman Empire joined Germany and Austria-Hungary. They were called the Central Powers.

After the German army moved almost to Paris, French defenses strengthened and stopped them in September 1914. Both sides became bogged down in a bloody conflict. Soldiers dug deep trenches into the ground, protecting themselves with barbed wire and machine guns. Inside the trenches, they lived in mud, suffered the lack of food, and were killed or wounded by exploding bombs. Attacks were even worse. Generals still hoped to win ground with massed attacks of huge armies. But, when soldiers left the trenches to storm enemy lines, they faced powerful weapons. Machine guns, tanks, poison gas, and larger pieces of artillery killed hundreds of thousands of soldiers. This was the war in France, which was called the Western Front.

The war on the Eastern Front showed more movement at first—but it was equally destructive. Russian armies attacked both Germany and Austria-Hungary. After some early success, they were driven back in both places. One reason was that Russia did not have a fully industrial economy. It could not keep troops supplied. Still, Russia had a huge population and could send millions to war. The large Russian army provided a constant threat to Germany, preventing it from putting its full resources against the allies in the west.

❸ A Global Conflict

KEY IDEA *World War I spread to several continents and used the full resources of many governments.*

The war moved into Southwest Asia when the Allies hoped to take a part of the Ottoman Empire called the Dardanelles. That would allow them to capture Constantinople—the Ottoman capital—and send supplies to Russia through the Black Sea. The attack failed with great loss of life. In another thrust at that empire, a British officer named T. E. Lawrence helped lead an Arab revolt against Ottoman rule. As a result, the Allies were able to capture several important cities in Southwest Asia.

Japan took German colonies in China and the Pacific Ocean. The Allies also captured three of the four German colonies in Africa. People in the Allies' colonies joined in the war effort. Some worked for the Allied cause. Others fought in the armies.

The British had used their strong navy to block all supplies from reaching Germany. In response, the Germans increased their submarine attacks on ships that brought food and supplies to the Allies. U.S. President Woodrow Wilson had protested this policy before, and did so again. When American ships were sunk, the American people grew angry. Then the British intercepted a secret message from Germany to Mexico. It offered to help Mexico regain land lost to the United States in the 1840s if Mexico allied itself with Germany. This and the submarine attacks turned many Americans against Germany. In April 1917, Congress declared war on Germany.

By that year, the war had had a terrible impact, killing millions and radically changing the lives of millions more—people at home as well as soldiers. This "Great War," as it was called, was a total war. It demanded all the resources of the countries that fought it. Governments took control of factories, telling them what to produce and how much of it to make. Governments rationed food and other goods, limiting how much people could buy and hold. That way they were sure to provide needed supplies to the armies in the field. They used propaganda to generate support for the war. They also took steps to put down any dissent against the war.

With so many men in the field, women played a growing role in the economies of the countries at war. They worked in factories, offices, and shops. They built planes and tanks, grew food and made clothing. These changes had an impact on people's attitudes toward what kind of work women could do.

In 1917, the United States entered the war, and Russia left it. Suffering during the war chipped away at the Russian people's support for the czar. In March, he stepped down. The new government hoped to continue fighting the war, but the Russian armies refused. Just months later, a new revolution struck. Communists seized Russia's government. They quickly made a treaty with Germany, giving up huge amounts of land in return for peace. In March 1918, Germany tried one final attack. Once again, the German army nearly reached Paris. The soldiers were tired, and supplies were short, though.

The Allies—now with fresh American troops—drove the Germans back.

Bulgaria and the Ottoman Empire surrendered. In October, a revolution toppled the emperor of Austria-Hungary. In November, Kaiser Wilhelm II was forced to step down in Germany. The new government agreed to stop fighting, and on November 11, 1918, Europe was finally at peace.

The war had made a great and terrible mark on the world. About 8.5 million soldiers had died and another 21 million had been wounded. Countless civilians had suffered as well. The economies of the warring nations had suffered serious damage, too. Farms were destroyed and factories ruined. One estimate said the war had caused $338 billion in damage.

Along with this death and destruction, the war had an emotional cost. People felt disillusioned since all the suffering did not seem to have a purpose. The art and literature of the years after the war reflected a new sense of hopelessness in people.

❹ A Flawed Peace

KEY IDEA *After winning the war, the Allies dictated a harsh peace that left many nations feeling betrayed.*

Many nations sent delegates to peace talks in Paris. The main leaders were Woodrow Wilson of the United States, Georges Clemenceau of France, and David Lloyd George of Britain. Germany and its allies and Russia were not present.

Wilson pushed for his peace plan called the Fourteen Points. He wanted to end secret treaties and alliances and give people the right to form their own nation. He also hoped to set up a world organization that could police the actions of nations and prevent future wars.

Britain and especially France had different views. They had suffered greatly in the war and wanted to punish Germany. After long debates, the leaders finally agreed on a peace settlement called the Treaty of Versailles.

The treaty called for a League of Nations—the world organization that Wilson wanted. It would include 32 nations, with the United States, Britain, France, Japan, and Italy making up the leadership. Germany and Russia were left out of the League. The treaty took away German land in Europe and took away its colonies. Limits were placed on the size of Germany's armed forces. Finally, Germany was given complete blame for the war, which meant it would have to make payments to the Allies for the damage caused.

Germany's former colonies were given to the Allies to govern until they decided which were ready for independence. Poland, Czechoslovakia, and Yugoslavia were all declared independent. Finland, Estonia, Latvia, and Lithuania—once part of Russia—were made independent nations as well. The Ottoman Empire was broken up. The Ottomans kept control only of Turkey.

The treaty never made a lasting peace. This was in part because the United States Senate never approved either the treaty or joining the League of Nations. Also, Germans bitterly resented the treaty, which placed all the blame for the war on them. Colonial peoples in Africa and Asia had hoped that they could win their independence. They were angry when the treaty did not allow for that. Japan and Italy were also upset with the treaty. They had both joined the war in hopes of winning more land and were disappointed by getting few territorial gains.

Review

Analyzing Causes and Recognizing Effects

1. What factors led to World War I?
2. Why did a revolution occur in Russia?
3. *Summarizing* What was the war like on the Western Front?
4. *Analyzing Issues* How did the war change the countries that fought it?
5. *Forming and Supporting Opinions* Discuss the weaknesses of the Treaty of Versailles.

Answer Key
Chapter 13
SUMMARY

The Great War, 1914–1918

Responses will vary but should include points similar to the following:

1. The factors leading to World War I included nationalism, which caused competition among nations; imperialism; the growing arms race and mobilization plans; and the system of alliances that pushed Europe into two armed camps.

2. The war on the Western Front was characterized by the suffering of trench warfare—with mud, starvation, disease, and constant bombardment—interrupted by occasional attacks that produced great death and destruction because of new war technologies.

3. World War I was a total war, and the people at home had to contribute to the war effort. It demanded all the resources of the countries that fought it. Governments took control of factories, rationed food and other goods, and used propaganda to generate support for the war. Women played a larger role in the economies of the countries at war, which changed people's ideas of what kind of work women could do.

4. A revolution took place in Russia because the czar did not respond to increasing calls for democracy, because the economy was in poor condition, because soldiers were tired of fighting, and because dedicated revolutionaries worked to bring about this revolution.

5. The Treaty of Versailles was imperfect because Germans resented it for being harsh, the League lost authority when the United States did not agree to join it, and people who did not win the right to self-determination were angry and disappointed by it.

CHAPTER
14
Summary

CHAPTERS IN BRIEF *Revolution and Nationalism,*
1900–1939

CHAPTER OVERVIEW *Old problems in Russia produced a revolution that resulted in the first Communist government. Joseph Stalin took control of the Soviet Union and became a dictator. Nationalists tried to gain control of China, but the country was plunged into decades of fighting. Nationalists pushed for self-government in India and won that right in Turkey, Iran, and Saudi Arabia.*

❶ Revolutions in Russia

KEY IDEA *Unrest in Russia erupted in revolution to produce the first Communist government.*

In 1881, reforms in Russia stopped when the czar was killed by radical students. The new czar, Alexander III, took back control of the Russian government. He cracked down on anyone who seemed to threaten his government. He also oppressed all non-Russian peoples who lived within the Russian empire, especially Jews.

In 1894, his son Nicholas II became czar and continued the strong rule. He launched a program aimed at building up Russia's industry. Russia quickly became a leading producer of steel in the world. However, this rapid industrial growth brought problems. Working conditions were poor, wages were low, and children were forced to work. Workers grew angry and often went on strike. Revolutionary groups wanted to topple the government. Some followed the teachings of Karl Marx. In 1903, they argued about how to carry out their revolution, and they split into two groups. One group—the Bolsheviks—was led by Vladimir Lenin. He fled Russia a few years later to await a better time to push his ideas.

Russia suffered a huge defeat at the hands of Japan in a war that started in 1904. In early 1905, the Russian army killed hundreds of hungry workers who had peacefully gathered to ask for relief. Strikes spread in protest, and Nicholas was forced to allow some reforms to take place.

The suffering caused by World War I was the final blow against the czar's rule. In just the first few months of war, Russia had four million soldiers killed, wounded, or captured. As the war worsened, the czar lost control of Russia. Soldiers refused to fight, prices shot sky high, and people starved. In March 1917, almost 200,000 workers took to the streets of one city to protest high prices. Soldiers shot into the crowd. Later they fired at their officers and joined the protest. The czar was forced to step down. A year later, he and his family were executed. A government led by Alexander Kerensky was formed.

Kerensky hoped to keep Russia in the war. The decision cost him the support of soldiers who wanted to fight no longer and workers and peasants who wanted an end to food shortages. Across the country these forces formed local councils called soviets. In some cities, the soviets actually had more real power than the government.

In the midst of this unrest, Lenin returned to Russia determined to bring about his revolution. His slogan "Peace, Land, and Bread" was soon taken up by many people. In November 1917, armed workers took control of government offices. The Kerensky reign was ended.

To win the peasants' support, Lenin ordered all farmland be given to them. Workers were given control of the factories. Soon Lenin agreed to a peace treaty with Germany. It gave away large amounts of Russian land, but it ended the war. Then, forces opposed to Lenin's revolution—supported by the Allies who fought Germany—tried to defeat Lenin's army in battle. The civil war lasted three years. The fighting and the famine that followed it killed 15 million Russians. In the end, though, Lenin's Red Army won.

In 1921, Lenin launched a new plan to rebuild the Russian economy. It allowed for some private ownership of property, relaxing Lenin's desire for complete state control. He also changed the government to form a new nation—the Soviet Union. It would be run by the leaders of the Communist Party. By the late 1920s, the Soviet economy had come back. Farms and factories were producing as much as they had before World War I.

❷ Totalitarianism
Case Study: Stalinist Russia

KEY IDEA *After Lenin died, Stalin seized power and transformed the Soviet Union into a totalitarian state.*

The term *totalitarian* describes a government that takes complete control over all parts of life in a country. This includes both public and private life. To keep everything under control totalitarian governments use several tactics. These include: police terror, propaganda, and persecution. The case study uses Joseph Stalin and Russia to show how a totalitarian state operates.

Joseph Stalin joined Lenin's revolutionary movement. Over time, he slowly built up his power. When Lenin died in 1924, Stalin took control of the Communist Party. He was less interested than Lenin in promoting revolution around the world. He wanted to increase the power of the Soviet Union. To achieve that, he built a totalitarian state. Government had total control over its people's lives.

Stalin kept tight control by creating a powerful secret police. In the mid-1930s, he turned against enemies—both real and imagined—within the Communist Party. Thousands were arrested and sent to exile or killed. Stalin also used propaganda to keep control. Official literature praised the government and its success. Any writings that expressed a different view were seized and their authors punished. Stalin's government also moved against religion. Churches were destroyed, and church leaders killed or sent into exile.

Stalin built a command economy—one in which the government makes all decisions of economic life. He pushed to complete the work of making the economy fully industrial. All resources were devoted to this effort. As a result, the Soviet people lacked food, housing, and clothing for many years. The plan did not meet Stalin's goals, but the industrial part of the economy did grow.

Stalin also launched a farming revolution. The government took control of the farms that people owned. It put them together in large, government-owned farms called collective farms. When peasants resisted, millions were killed, and millions more were sent to Siberia. With these brutal methods, Stalin got farm output to rise.

Stalin completely changed Soviet society. Women enjoyed equal rights—though rights were few. They filled all kinds of jobs on the farms and in factories.

They studied for careers that had been closed to them before. People in general were more educated.

❸ Imperial China Collapses

KEY IDEA *After the fall of the Qing Dynasty, nationalists and communists struggled for power.*

Unrest also plagued China. Many Chinese resented the great control that foreign nations had over their economy. Some wanted to modernize China so it could regain power. One of the leaders of this push was Sun Yixian. His group was called the Kuomintang, or Nationalist Party. In 1912, he led a revolt that toppled the Qing Dynasty and was made the president of the new republic.

Sun had three main principles. He wanted political and economic rights for all Chinese people and an end to foreign control of China. Sun turned over his presidency six weeks later to Yuan Shikai, who became a military dictator. After Yuan died in 1916, civil war broke out. The people suffered terribly from famine and brutal attacks. Sun could not reorganize his Kuomintang.

China's leaders hoped to win the support of the Allies during World War I. They declared war on Germany. When the war ended, though, they were disappointed. Instead of giving China freedom from foreign influence, the Treaty of Versailles merely changed masters. The parts of China that had been controlled by Germany were handed over to Japan. Angry Chinese protested.

In the 1920s, rebels began to look to Marxism and the Russian Revolution for a solution to China's problems. The Communist Party in China was organized. One of the leaders was Mao Zedong. The Communists joined with the Kuomintang. Sun died in 1925, and Jiang Jieshi became leader of the Kuomintang. Many in the party were business people. They now feared Communist ideas about government control of economic life. Jiang agreed with them.

Jiang did not move against the Communists at first. In 1927, though, his forces struck against them. Only a few Communists survived, and they were forced into hiding. In 1928, Jiang became president of China. Soon China was torn by a civil war between the remaining Communists and Jiang's forces.

The Communists, under Mao Zedong, moved to south-central China. They built an army of peasants that struck quickly against Jiang's forces. In 1933, Jiang's army completely surrounded them. But the Communists sneaked away on a famous Long March of 6,000 miles to the north. Thousands died, but the Communists survived, hiding in caves.

At the same time, China had other problems. In 1931, Japan invaded the part of China called Manchuria. They took control there and six years later began a new invasion of other areas. They were able to quickly seize large parts of the country. With this new threat, Jiang and the Communists agreed to join together to fight the Japanese.

❹ Nationalism in India and Southwest Asia

KEY IDEA *Nationalism triggered independence movements to overthrow colonial power.*

Many Indians of the upper classes were educated in British schools. They learned the Western ideals of nationalism and democracy. They also grew angry at British domination of Indian life. Some formed into two groups, the Congress Party and the Muslim League.

More than a million Indians served in the British army in World War I. The British promised to make changes to the government of India that would give the Indian people greater control of their own nation. After the war, though, returning Indian soldiers were once again treated as second-class citizens. Reforms were not made. When Indians protested, the British Parliament passed a law that allowed protesters to be jailed without a trial. Indians were further enraged. About 10,000 Indians gathered to protest this act. The British had also banned such public meetings, but the crowd was mostly unaware of that fact. British troops fired on the crowd, killing several hundred. The massacre at Amritsar sparked further protests.

Mohandas K. Gandhi became the leader of India's protest movement. He organized a widespread campaign of noncooperation with the British and passive resistance to unjust laws. He asked Indians to stop buying British goods, attending British schools, paying British taxes, or voting in British-run elections. He also convinced his followers to take these actions without using violence.

British jails filled with thousands of Indians who broke British laws in order to protest them.

Indians resented a British law that forced them to buy salt only from the government. Gandhi organized a huge march to the sea to make salt by evaporating sea water. At a related march, police beat many people protesting the salt tax. In 1935, the British finally gave in. They passed a law that allowed local Indian limited self-government. Though they had met some success, Indians had other problems. Tensions between Hindus and Muslims were high.

Other changes took place in Southwest Asia. Mustafa Kemal, a military commander, became the leader of a new republic in Turkey. He took many steps to modernize society and the economy in Turkey. He loosened Islam's hold on Turkish law. Another commander led a revolt in Persia that won independence from Britain in that land. He also modernized his country, and he changed its name to Iran. In both Turkey and Iran, women gained new rights. A new leader also emerged in Arabia. He united different groups into one kingdom, which he called Saudi Arabia. While he took steps to modernize life in his land, he kept the traditional practices of Islam strong.

Starting in the 1920s, Southwest Asia saw a major new economic change. Western companies discovered large reserves of oil in several countries in this part of the world. Oil brought huge sums of money to these countries. The desire to tap into this wealth also persuaded Western countries to try to gain power in the area.

Review

1. ***Drawing Conclusions*** How did the problems of the early 1900s lead to the Russian Revolution?
2. ***Comparing and Contrasting*** Compare Kerensky's and Lenin's plans.
3. ***Summarizing*** In what ways was Stalin's government an example of totalitarian rule?
4. ***Analyzing Causes and Recognizing Effects*** How did the Treaty of Versailles add to China's problems?
5. ***Determining Main Ideas*** Explain Gandhi's ideas of noncooperation and nonviolent protest.

Answer Key
Chapter 14
SUMMARY

Revolution and Nationalism, 1900–1939

Responses will vary but should include points similar to the following:

1. Rapid industrial growth in Russia in the early 1900s resulted in poor working conditions, low wages, and angry workers who often went on strike. Rebels formed revolutionary groups that wanted to topple the government. The war against Japan led to a demonstration that resulted in soldiers firing into the crowd. Strikes and violence spread in protest.

2. Kerensky wanted to continue the war, which cost him the support of soldiers and of workers and peasants who wanted an end to food shortages. Lenin urged "Peace, Land, and Bread"—an end to the war to win the favor of the soldiers, and food and land to win the masses.

3. Stalin controlled all aspects of people's lives. He devoted all economic resources to making the economy fully industrial, even though it meant shortages of consumer goods for people. He forced farmers to organize farms and killed those who resisted. He used secret police to remove rebels or enemies in the party. He censored ideas that he did not like.

4. Chinese leaders had hoped to win their freedom from European control by declaring war on Germany. Instead of getting freedom, though, China suffered. Parts of China that Germany had controlled were simply handed over to Japan. This led to widespread discontent.

5. With noncooperation, Gandhi wanted Indians to stop buying British goods, attending British schools, paying British taxes, or voting in British-run elections. By nonviolence, he wanted Indians to protest British laws on purpose in order to protest them but not to resort to destruction of property or injuring of people.

CHAPTER

15

Summary

CHAPTERS IN BRIEF *Years of Crisis, 1919–1939*

CHAPTER OVERVIEW After World War I, new ideas and technologies changed old ways of thinking and living. The economic collapse called the Great Depression tested weak democratic governments in Europe. This crisis helped bring dictators to power in eastern Europe in the 1930s. Meanwhile, Japan, Germany, and Italy took actions that would soon plunge the world into another war.

❶ Postwar Uncertainty

KEY IDEA The postwar period was one of loss and uncertainty but also one of invention and creativity.

Two thinkers developed radical new ideas that challenged old ways of thinking. Albert Einstein revolutionized physics with his ideas about space, time, matter, and energy. He said that as moving objects neared the speed of light, space and time become relative. That means they change. His idea is the theory of relativity. Sigmund Freud's work changed the way people thought about the human mind. He said that much of human behavior was irrational—due to urges and desires buried in the unconscious mind of each person. Though resisted at first, Freud's ideas gained wide influence.

Looking at the destruction of World War I, many philosophers lost faith in reason and progress. One group of them was called existentialists. They argued that there is no universal meaning to the world. Each person must give it his or her own meaning through actions taken. They were influenced by Friedrich Nietzsche, a German philosopher of the late 1800s. He said that reason, democracy, and progress were empty ideas. He urged people to adopt the values of pride and strength.

Some writers, like Franz Kafka, showed the horrors of modern life. His novels put people in threatening situations that they could not understand or escape.

Artists rebelled against traditional painting. They did not merely re-create realistic objects. Paul Klee used bold colors and distorted lines. Pablo Picasso founded a style called Cubism that broke objects into geometric shapes. Painters called surrealists showed a dreamlike existence outside of reality.

Composers created a new style of music. Some, like Igor Stravinsky, used unusual rhythms or harsh, rather than pleasing, sounds. African-American musicians in the United States developed a lively, loose form of popular music called jazz.

Society changed after World War I as well. Young people experimented with modern values. Women set aside earlier forms of dress, wearing new styles that were looser and shorter. Many women also began to work in new careers.

Technology brought about changes to society as well. Improvements to the automobile helped make cars more desirable and affordable. As a result, more and more people bought cars. They began to move to suburbs outside cities, using their cars to travel to work. The auto boom also gave a boost to some industries. Another change was the growth in air travel. American pilot Charles Lindbergh caught the world's attention when he flew alone across the Atlantic Ocean in 1927. In 1932, Amelia Earhart became the first woman to make the flight alone.

The radio developed during World War I. In the 1920s, large radio networks were built. They offered programs such as news, plays, comedies, and sports. Soon millions of people were entertained by radios in their homes. Millions more went to movie theaters to watch motion pictures. Movies were produced all over the world, especially in southern California.

❷ A Worldwide Depression

KEY IDEA An economic depression in the United States spread to the world and lasted a decade.

After the war, European countries were in bad shape. European influence in world affairs was declining. The new republics that had formed out of the old empires of Europe often had shaky governments. Even nations that had had democracy for many years experienced problems. They had so many political parties that no one party could rule alone. There were so many governments formed that it was difficult to develop policies.

The situation was worst in Germany. The people felt little loyalty to the government, and the economy was weak. Prices rose sharply, and money lost its value. An American drew up a plan that used American bank loans to help the German economy recover. By 1929, German factories produced as much as they had before the war.

World nations also took steps to try to ensure peace. France and Germany promised never to attack one another. Most countries of the world signed a treaty in which they pledged not to use war to gain their goals. There was no way to enforce the treaty, however, which made it weak.

The economy of the United States enjoyed a boom in the 1920s. But this growth hid problems. Workers were unable to buy all the goods produced, and when their purchases slowed, factories slowed production. Farmers faced falling food prices and slow sales. They were unable to repay loans and lost their farms. In 1929, stock prices in the United States plunged. The Great Depression was on.

The American Depression hit other countries. Nations raised tariffs—taxes on goods imported from other countries—to keep import prices high. They wanted to increase sales by local companies. But it all backfired. Trade between nations dropped, and unemployment shot up in many countries. The world suffered, including Latin America. As world trade went down, few countries bought the sugar, beef, and copper they produced.

Each country met the economic crisis in its own way. In Britain, a new multiparty government took over. It took steps that slowly improved the economy and cut unemployment. By 1937, production was up again. In France, after several governments lost support, moderates and Socialists combined to form a government. It passed laws to help workers, but companies raised prices to cover their costs. As a result, unemployment was still high.

In Sweden, Norway, and Denmark, the governments played active roles in the economy. They taxed people with jobs to have money to pay benefits to people without jobs. The governments also created jobs by hiring out-of-work people to build roads and buildings.

In the United States, Franklin D. Roosevelt became president in 1932. He began a program that he called the New Deal. The government began large public works projects. This effort created jobs for millions. Businesses and farmers also got help from the government. The American economy got better but the recovery was slow.

❸ Fascism Rises in Europe

KEY IDEA *Because of political and economic problems, Italy and Germany turned to dictators.*

In other countries, the economic crisis of the Great Depression led to the loss of democracy. There, millions of people turned to strong rulers to try to solve their economic problems. These tough leaders followed a set of beliefs called fascism. Fascist leaders were strongly nationalist. They believed in strength and power and built strong military forces. Fascist governments were controlled by one party, and that party was dominated by one leader. The leader was the nation's dictator. Fascist governments did not give any rights to their people.

Fascism arose in Italy because people there were angry that the treaty that came after World War I did not give them more gains in territory. Also, people with more money feared that unrest in Italy would result in a Communist government, as had happened in Russia. Benito Mussolini rose to power promising to revive the economy and armed forces of Italy. He used armed thugs who made threats to political opponents. The king of Italy was forced to let Mussolini lead the government.

Another Fascist arose in Germany. Adolf Hitler was the leader of the Nazi Party. He tried to take control of the government of Germany in 1923, but the attempt failed. He was sent to prison, where he wrote a book that summarized his ideas. Hitler believed that Germans were superior to all other people. He said that the Treaty of Versailles treated Germany unfairly, and that a crowded Germany needed the lands of eastern Europe and Russia. When the Depression hit Germany, the country was in terrible shape. Hitler was named leader of the German government but soon took the powers of a dictator. All those who opposed him were arrested. His economic program gave work to millions but took away their rights to organize into unions or to strike. He took control of all areas of life. He burned books that went against Nazi ideas and forced children to join Nazi groups. Hitler also launched attacks on Germany's Jews. Laws took away their rights. In November 1938, mobs destroyed thousands of Jewish-owned buildings and attacked Jewish people.

Dictators took control in other countries as well. Hungary, Poland, Yugoslavia, Albania, Bulgaria, and Romania all had dictators—or kings who ruled like dictators. Only Czechoslovakia remained as a democracy in eastern Europe.

❹ Aggressors Invade Nations

KEY IDEA *As Germany, Italy, and Japan conquered other countries, the rest of the world did nothing.*

In the 1930s, the major democracies—Britain, France, and the United States—still faced serious problems at home. Dictators in Germany and Italy took advantage of this and began moving to gain territory. So, too, did Japan, now ruled by generals. These military leaders had taken power when the Depression struck. They planned to capture China as a part of a Pacific empire.

In 1931, the Japanese army captured Manchuria, a part of China. It was rich in coal and iron and as a result provided valuable resources for the Japanese economy. Other countries protested in the League of Nations but did nothing else. Japan ignored the protests and in 1933 pulled out of the League. It stayed in Manchuria, though. Four years later, Japan invaded China. The strong Japanese army swept Chinese fighters aside. It killed tens of thousands of Chinese in the city of Nanjing. Chinese forces—both the Nationalists of the government and Communist rebels—continued to fight Japan.

Italy's Mussolini wanted an Italian empire in Africa, and in 1935 he invaded Ethiopia. His troops won easy victory. Haile Selassie, the emperor of Ethiopia, pleaded to the League of Nations for help. The League did nothing.

Hitler made moves also. He broke the Versailles Treaty by rebuilding Germany's army. In 1936, he sent troops into an area of Germany that the treaty had forbidden them to enter. France and Britain again refused to stand up to Germany. This move won Hitler more support in Germany. That year, he signed an agreement with Mussolini and also with Japan. The three nations were called the Axis Powers.

In 1936, Spain erupted in civil war as the army revolted against a leftist government. Hitler and Mussolini sent aid to the army, which was backed by Spanish Fascists. The Soviet Union sent aid to the government. In 1939, the army won and Francisco Franco became Spain's Fascist dictator.

In March 1938, Hitler moved his troops into Austria. He made it part of Germany, breaking the Versailles Treaty again. France and Britain once more did nothing. The next year, Hitler demanded that Czechoslovakia give up part of its land to Germany. The country refused, but Britain and France agreed to allow Germany to take the land. Hitler promised to respect the new borders of Czechoslovakia, but a few months later he took the entire country.

In the summer of 1939, Hitler made a similar demand of Poland. That nation also refused to give up land. Britain and France now said that they would protect Poland. But Hitler guessed they would not back this up. Meanwhile, he made an agreement with Soviet dictator Joseph Stalin in which the two countries promised never to attack each other.

Review

Clarifying

1. What ideas of Einstein and Freud challenged old ways of thinking?
2. How did technology change society after the war?
3. ***Comparing and Contrasting*** Compare the French approach to the Depression with the New Deal.
4. ***Analyzing Causes and Recognizing Effects*** What European nations came to be ruled by dictators, and why?
5. ***Following Chronological Order*** Describe the sequence of events in the 1930s that led to war.

Answer Key
Chapter 15
SUMMARY

Years of Crisis, 1919–1939

Responses will vary but should include points similar to the following:

1. Einstein's new physics made people see the world differently. Freud's theories about the unconscious mind undercut people's faith in reason, which was reflected in philosophy and art. Artists, writers, and musicians all broke with traditional forms and styles of expression.

2. The automobile boom changed society by making people more mobile and sending more of them to live in the suburbs and to travel by car. New technologies such as the radio and movies created mass entertainment media.

3. In France, the government tried to pass laws that would benefit workers, but the companies simply raised prices to cover their higher costs. As a result, unemployment did not go down. In the United States, the New Deal created new jobs in public works programs, but not enough to make the economy recover completely.

4. Dictators took control of Italy, Germany, and all the nations of eastern Europe except Czechoslovakia. They took advantage of people's resentment over the terms of the Treaty of Versailles, fears of communism, economic troubles of the Depression, and their own strong-arm tactics that suppressed opposition.

5. 1931: Japan invades Manchuria. 1933: Japan pulls out of the League of Nations. 1935: Mussolini invades Ethiopia. 1936: Hitler sends troops into areas where Germany was forbidden to put them. 1936: Germany, Italy, and Japan sign agreement. 1936–1939: Spanish Civil War; Fascists are supported by Germany and Italy. 1937: Japan invades China. 1938: Hitler moves troops into Austria. 1939: Hitler takes Czechoslovakia. 1939: Hitler threatens Poland; 1939: Hitler and Stalin sign treaty in which each promises not to attack the other.

CHAPTERS IN BRIEF *World War II, 1939–1945*

CHAPTER 16 Summary

CHAPTER OVERVIEW *Germany's Adolf Hitler began World War II, which the United States entered after a Japanese attack on a U.S. naval base. Hitler's racial hatred resulted in the deaths of millions of people, many of them Jews. After years of struggle, the Allies won the war, but millions had died and large parts of Europe and Japan were destroyed.*

❶ Hitler's Lightning War

KEY IDEA *Using sudden, mass attacks, Germany over-ran much of Europe and North Africa.*

In 1939, having conquered Austria and Czechoslovakia, Adolf Hitler decided to move on Poland. He had signed an agreement with Stalin of the Soviet Union. In it, they agreed to split Poland between them. This deal removed the threat of the Soviets attacking Germany from the east.

So, on September 1, the German army invaded Poland. Using planes, tanks, and troops, it moved suddenly in a technique called blitzkrieg—"lightning war." Britain and France declared war, but Poland fell before they could help. On September 17, Stalin invaded Finland and eastern Poland.

In April 1940, Hitler's armies conquered Denmark and Norway. Within two months, they also captured Belgium, the Netherlands, Luxembourg, and France. Some French, led by Charles de Gaulle, escaped to Britain to continue fighting. By then, Italy's Benito Mussolini had joined Hitler's side.

Great Britain—now led by Winston Churchill—stood alone. To prepare for an invasion of Britain, the German air force launched bombing attacks to weaken the country. The British air force fought back. It was helped by the newly developed radar that warned of coming attacks. Also, the British had broken the German army's secret code. The air war over Britain lasted many months. Unable to break British defenses, Hitler called off the attacks.

He next turned to the Mediterranean and the east. Germany sent troops to North Africa, where its ally, Italy, was losing to British forces. German troops joined the battle and fought a seesaw struggle with the British. Hitler forced Bulgaria, Romania, and Hungary to join Germany in the war. In April 1941, German armies quickly took control of Yugoslavia and Greece. In June, Hitler turned on his one-time ally and launched a surprise invasion of the Soviet Union. The Red Army, though the largest in the world, was not well-equipped or well-trained. The Germans quickly pushed deep into Soviet land. As the Red Army was forced to retreat, it destroyed everything left behind to keep supplies out of German hands. Stopped from taking Leningrad in the north, the Germans turned on Moscow, the Soviet capital. A strong Soviet counterattack, combined with fierce Russian winter weather, forced the Germans back.

The United States watched these events. Many Americans did not want to join in the war. President Roosevelt wanted to help the Allies, however. He persuaded Congress to allow Britain and France to buy American weapons. Soon American ships were escorting British cargo ships carrying guns. By the fall of 1941, U.S. ships had orders to fire on German submarines. The United States and Germany had an undeclared naval war.

Roosevelt met with Churchill in August of 1941. Although the United States was not officially in the war, the two leaders issued a statement called the Atlantic Charter. It supported free trade and the right of people to form their own national government.

❷ Japan's Pacific Campaign

KEY IDEA *Japan attacked Pearl Harbor in Hawaii and brought the United States into World War II.*

The military leaders who ran the Japanese government also had plans to build an empire. They captured part of China in 1931. In 1937, they invaded the center of China but met strong resistance. Needing resources for this war, they decided to move into Southeast Asia. The United States feared that Japanese control of this area would threaten U.S. holdings in the Pacific. Roosevelt gave military aid to China and cut off oil shipments to Japan. The Japanese decided to attack the United States.

On December 7, 1941, the Japanese navy began a surprise attack on the U.S. Navy base at Pearl Harbor in Hawaii. In just two hours, Japanese planes sank a major part of the U.S. Pacific Fleet. The next day, Congress declared war on Japan. The attack on Pearl Harbor was just one of many sudden strikes. Japan also captured Guam and Wake Islands, and the Philippines. It took Indonesia from the Dutch and Hong Kong, Malaya, and Singapore from the British.

In April 1942, the United States sent planes to drop bombs on Tokyo. The attack raised the morale of Americans. In May 1942, at the Battle of the Coral Sea, the Allies suffered heavy losses but were able to stop the Japanese advance and save Australia. The next month, the U.S. Navy scored an important victory near Midway Island in the central Pacific. In this battle, Japan lost four aircraft carriers, the most important naval weapon in the war. The victory turned the tide of war against Japan.

The United States now went on the attack. General Douglas MacArthur proposed hopping past the strongly defended Japanese-held islands. He wanted to attack weaker ones. The first attack came at Guadalcanal, in the Solomon Islands, where the Japanese were building an air base. However, it took six months for U.S. and Australian troops to clear Japanese soldiers off the island.

❸ The Holocaust

KEY IDEA *During the Holocaust, Hitler's Nazis killed six million Jews and millions of other "non-Aryans."*

Part of Hitler's new order for Europe included getting rid of "inferior" people. Hitler believed in a German "master race." He had a deep-seated hatred of people who were not German and especially of Jews. He and his Nazis made persecution of Jews government policy.

During the 1930s, Hitler passed laws that took away the rights of German Jews. One night in November 1938, Nazi mobs attacked Jews throughout Germany. They destroyed homes and businesses and killed or beat many people. Thousands of Jews tried to leave Germany. Other countries accepted a large number but were unwilling to take all those who wished to leave. Hitler ordered all Jews in Germany and his conquered lands to live in certain parts of cities called ghettos.

Hitler took steps to kill as many Jews as possible. The plan was the "Final Solution" to what the Nazis called the "Jewish problem." Germans also turned on many other people—Roma (gypsies), Poles, Russians, and those who were mentally or physically disabled. The Germans put the most attention on Jews, however.

Thousands of Jews were shot to death by "killing squads." Millions were gathered and placed in concentration camps. These prisons used the inmates as slave workers. Many in the camps died of starvation or disease. Starting in 1942, the Nazis built "death camps." At these camps, thousands of Jews were gassed to death in huge gas chambers. In the end, six million Jews were killed by the Nazis. Fewer than four million European Jews survived.

❹ The Allied Victory

KEY IDEA *The United States, Great Britain, and the Soviet Union scored key victories and won the war.*

In 1942, Roosevelt, Churchill, and Stalin planned the Allies' strategy. Stalin wanted Britain and the United States to attack Germany to relieve the pressure on his armies. They agreed but chose to attack in North Africa. In late 1942, the British army drove the Germans out of Egypt and back to the west. Meanwhile, American troops landed behind the Germans and began moving east. The Germans were finally forced to abandon Africa in May 1943.

At the same time, the Soviets enjoyed a major victory. German troops had invaded the Soviet city of Stalingrad in 1942. The Red Army forced the Germans to surrender in February 1943.

American and British soldiers next invaded Italy and captured Sicily. Mussolini was forced from power and the new Italian government surrendered. Hitler was unwilling to give up Italy. His army fought fiercely there until 1945.

While the Allied armies fought, people at home suffered. Some British and Soviet citizens died. In the United States, citizens faced shortages. Goods such as food, tires, gasoline, and clothing were in short supply. The government rationed these items—limiting how much a person could have—to make sure that there were enough for the armies.

Some Americans were even imprisoned. Since bitter feelings against the Japanese became widespread, mistrust of Americans of Japanese heritage grew. The U.S. government gathered thousands of Japanese Americans who lived on the West Coast and forced them to move to concentration camps in the western United States. Two-thirds of them were American citizens.

In early 1944, the Allies built a massive force to retake France. In June, an invasion of thousands of ships, planes, and soldiers was launched. The Allies suffered heavy losses but gained control of northern France. A month later, Allied forces broke out and began to pour through German lines. By September, the Allies had forced the Germans out of France, Belgium, Luxembourg, and much of the Netherlands.

At the same time, the Soviets were pushing the Germans back in eastern Europe. In late 1944, Hitler ordered his army to make one final, large-scale attack in the west. In the Battle of the Bulge, it punched through Allied lines until an Allied counterattack forced it back to Germany. By late April 1945, Soviet troops surrounded Berlin, Hitler's headquarters. Hitler killed himself, and a week later, the Germans surrendered. Roosevelt had not lived to see this victory, however. He had died in early April. Harry Truman was now president.

In the Pacific, the Allies advanced on Japanese territory starting in 1943. By the fall of 1944, they had landed troops in the Philippines. The Japanese sent their remaining ships to try to destroy the U.S. Navy near the Philippines. In the Battle of Leyte Gulf, in October 1944, the Japanese lost badly, and their navy was crushed. American troops began to move closer to Japan. In March 1945, they captured an island called Iwo Jima. By June, they had won control of Okinawa, an island just 350 miles from Japan.

Japan was the next stop. But the U.S. military feared that an invasion of Japan would cost half a million Allied lives. In August, President Truman ordered an experimental atomic bomb dropped on the city of Hiroshima to try to quickly end the war. Three days later, a second bomb was dropped on Nagasaki. Tens of thousands of Japanese died. In September, Japan surrendered.

❺ Europe and Japan in Ruins

KEY IDEA *World War II cost millions of lives and billions of dollars in damage. It left Europe and Japan in ruins.*

The war had left Europe in ruins, with about 60 million dead and hundreds of cities destroyed. Suffering continued for many years in Europe.

The old Fascist governments had disappeared. At first, the Communist parties grew strong in France and Italy. People who opposed communism grew alarmed. They voted leaders from other parties into power. When the economies of these lands improved, communism lost appeal. During efforts to rebuild Europe, the Allies held trials in the city of Nuremberg, Germany. There, captured Nazi leaders were charged with crimes against humanity. They were found guilty, and some were executed.

The U.S. Army occupied Japan under the command of General MacArthur. He disbanded the Japanese army and took steps to give farmers and workers more power in the economy. He led the effort to write a new constitution for Japan, which changed how the Japanese viewed the world. The emperor was forced to declare that he was not a god. The new constitution gave all power to the Japanese people, who voted for members of a parliament that would rule the land. All Japanese over age 20—including women—were given the right to vote. In 1951, other nations finally signed a formal peace with Japan. A few months later, U.S. military occupation ended.

Review

1. **Summarizing** What was the first stop to Hitler? How did it affect later events?
2. **Analyzing Causes** What led to tensions between the United States and Japan before war broke out?
3. **Recognizing Effects** How did the American occupation change Japan?
4. **Following Chronological Order** Outline the fate of European Jews from the early 1930s to the Holocaust.
5. **Forming and Supporting Opinions** Do you think it was justified to drop the atomic bomb on Japanese cities? Explain your answer.

Answer Key
Chapter 16
SUMMARY

World War II, 1939–1945

Responses will vary but should include points similar to the following:

1. The first stop to Hitler's advances was the Battle of Britain, in which he was unable to weaken Great Britain enough for an invasion. His failure there led to an attack on the Soviet Union, which he was unable to conquer.

2. Japan hoped to expand its holdings in Southeast Asia, which the United States feared would threaten its own colonies in the Pacific. The United States imposed an oil embargo on Japan, which angered the Japanese.

3. At first, German Jews lost their rights. Then they were attacked by mobs. Next Jews in Germany and conquered lands were ordered to live in ghettos. Many were shot to death by killing squads. Finally, they were systematically put into camps as slave workers and then put into "death camps" and killed.

4. Was justified: American military leaders believed that an invasion of Japan would cost half a million American lives. They had a responsibility to protect their soldiers' lives. Was not justified: The atomic bomb was a terrible weapon, and an attack that led to the deaths of tens of thousands of civilians is not justified.

5. The American occupation resulted in the Japanese emperor acknowledging that he was not a god, in a major change to the government of Japan, and in economic changes that gave farmers and workers more power in Japanese society.

CHAPTER 17
Summary

CHAPTERS IN BRIEF *Restructuring the Postwar World, 1945–Present*

CHAPTER OVERVIEW *The United States and Soviet Union opposed each other as they tried to achieve different goals. Communists won a civil war in China, making it the world's second Communist nation. The United States fought two wars in Asia trying to contain communism. The Cold War also spread to Latin America and elsewhere. The superpowers later began to enjoy better relations.*

❶ Cold War: Superpowers Face Off

KEY IDEA *The conflicting aims of the United States and the Soviet Union led to global competition.*

The United States and the Soviet Union were allies during World War II. In February 1945, they agreed that Germany would be divided into separate zones. Each zone would be occupied by the soldiers of one of the main Allied powers. They also agreed that Germany would have to repay the Soviet Union for damage and loss of life. Soviet leader Joseph Stalin, in turn, promised free elections in Eastern Europe and to declare war on Japan. These allies also were among 50 countries that formed the United Nations in 1945. This new world body was pledged to save the world from war.

Still, the two superpowers had sharp political and economic differences. They also had different goals after the war. The United States wanted to encourage democracy and trade. It wanted to put the different zones of Germany back together to make one nation. The Soviet Union had these goals: to promote communism, to take advantage of raw materials in Eastern Europe and rebuild its own economy, and to keep Germany divided and weak.

After the war, Stalin made sure Communist governments were in place in Eastern Europe. This divided Europe between the Communist East and the democratic West. This division was called the "iron curtain." U.S. President Harry Truman then began a policy of containment to block further Soviet expansion. As part of this policy, the United States adopted the Marshall Plan in 1947. The plan donated food and materials such as machines to European countries, helping them rebuild from war.

In 1948, the Soviets and Americans clashed over Germany. France, Britain, and the United States agreed to pull their troops out of Germany and let the three zones that they occupied unite. The Soviets refused to leave their zone, however. Then they cut off all highway and train traffic into Berlin, which was deep within the Soviet zone. The United States and British responded with the Berlin Airlift. They flew food and supplies into the city for 11 months. Finally, the Soviets lifted the blockade.

The growing struggle between Americans and Soviets came to be called the Cold War. Many other countries allied with one superpower or another. The United States, Canada, and several countries in Western Europe formed the North Atlantic Treaty Organization (NATO). In this military alliance, each nation promised to defend any other member that was attacked. The Soviets and the countries of Eastern Europe made a similar agreement. It was called the Warsaw Pact.

In 1949, the Soviet Union announced that it, like the United States, had developed an atomic bomb. Three years later, both superpowers had a newer, even more deadly weapon—the hydrogen bomb. Soon both nations were involved in an arms race, as they produced growing numbers of nuclear weapons and developed new ways to deliver them.

In 1957, Soviet scientists shocked the world by launching *Sputnik*, the world's first human-made satellite. Many Americans felt that the Soviets were far ahead in science and technology. The United States then began spending huge amounts of money to improve science education.

❷ Communists Take Power in China

KEY IDEA *Chinese Communists defeated Nationalist forces, and two separate Chinas emerged.*

Nationalists and Communists fought for control of China in the 1930s. When Japan invaded China, the two sides joined to fight the common enemy. After World War II, they began fighting each other again. Their renewed war lasted from 1946 to 1949. The Communists won because their troops were well-trained in guerrilla war. They also enjoyed the backing of the peasants to whom they had promised land. In 1949, Jiang Jieshi and other Nationalist leaders fled to the island of Taiwan. The United States helped Jiang set up a new government there. The Nationalists called their land the Republic of China. The Soviets helped Mao Zedong and his government, the People's Republic of China.

Mao began to rebuild China. He seized land and gave it to the peasants. But he also forced the peasants—in groups of 200 to 300 households—to join collective farms. The people on each of these farms were given the land as a group. He also took control of China's industries. Under Mao's plan, production of industrial products went up.

With this success, Mao launched the "Great Leap Forward." He wanted to make the collective farms larger and more productive. The plan failed. People did not like strong government control. Planning by the government was not good. Poor weather produced a famine that killed millions.

After this failure, Mao played a smaller role in the government. He grew unhappy with the direction the country was taking, however. In 1966, he launched the Cultural Revolution. Using young students formed into groups called Red Guards, Mao tried to revive the revolutionary spirit in China. The Red Guards struck at teachers, scientists, and artists. They shut down schools and sent intellectuals to the country to work on farms. They killed thousands of people who resisted. China was in chaos, with factories shut down and farm production dropping. Eventually, Mao finally put an end to the Cultural Revolution.

❸ Wars in Korea and Vietnam

KEY IDEA *In Asia, the Cold War flared into actual wars supported mainly by the superpowers.*

After World War II, Korea was divided into a Soviet-backed north and an American-supported south. On June 25, 1950, North Korea invaded the South. President Truman fought this move with United Nations help. The United States and other countries sent troops to assist South Korea. At first, the North Korean army captured almost all of South Korea. Then the UN army began a bold counterattack. In just two months, it had pushed the North Koreans far back, nearly to

China. The Chinese then entered the war and drove the UN forces back. Bitter fighting continued until 1953. That year, the two Koreas agreed to a ceasefire. The earlier boundary splitting North and South Korea at the 38th parallel remained the same.

North Korea developed as a Communist country following the war. It had a strong army and tight government control, but it also had many economic problems. South Korea's economy grew, in part because it received U.S. aid. However, for more than 30 years, dictators ruled the country. Free elections were held only after a new constitution was accepted in 1987.

The United States faced another war against Communists, this time in Vietnam. That area had been a French colony until Japan invaded it early in World War II. When Japan lost, the French returned. A Vietnamese nationalist named Ho Chi Minh wanted to win independence. First, he drove the French out of Vietnam. A peace conference split Vietnam in two, with Ho taking charge in North Vietnam. He made it a Communist state. Communist rebels—the Vietcong—stayed active in the South.

Seeing that the government of South Vietnam was threatened by Communists, the United States began to send large numbers of soldiers. First it sent advisers, later combat troops. By 1968, more than 500,000 U.S. troops were there. They could not win the war on the ground. The United States also tried bombing or burning forests in the South to drive the Vietcong from their hiding places. These actions made peasants in the South more likely to support the North. Many in the United States came to oppose the war.

In the late 1960s, President Richard Nixon began to cut the number of U.S. troops in Vietnam in order to turn the fighting over to the South Vietnamese. The last American troops left in 1973. Two years later, North Vietnam overran the South and made Vietnam one country again. About 1.5 million people fled Vietnam. Today, Vietnam remains Communist but is looking for other nations to invest in its economy.

Fighting in Vietnam spilled over into its neighbor Cambodia. Rebels there set up a brutal Communist government. It killed 2 million people and imposed its will. In 1978, the Vietnamese invaded the country, overthrowing the rebels. Vietnam withdrew in 1989. In 1993, Cambodia held free elections.

❹ The Cold War Divides the World

KEY IDEA *The superpowers supported opposing sides in Latin American and Middle Eastern conflicts.*

After World War II, many nations in Africa, Asia, and Latin America had serious problems. They were plagued by ethnic conflict, lack of education and technology, poverty, and political unrest. Some of these countries tried to stay neutral in the Cold War. Others actively sought American or Soviet aid.

In Cuba, the United States supported a dictator in the 1950s. In 1959, a young lawyer, Fidel Castro, led a successful revolt. Castro then turned to the Soviets for aid. In 1962, the Soviets and Americans almost went to war over Soviet nuclear missiles placed in Cuba. The Soviets finally pulled the missiles out. Over time, the Cuban economy became more dependent on Soviet aid. When the Soviet Union dropped communism in 1991, this aid stopped. It was a serious blow to Cuba's economy.

The United States had also backed a dictator in Nicaragua. He fell in 1979 to Communist rebels. When the new government began helping leftist rebels in nearby El Salvador, the United States struck back. It began to support forces in Nicaragua that wanted to overthrow the Communists. The civil war lasted more than a decade. Finally, the different sides agreed to hold free elections.

The Middle East often saw conflict between those who wanted a modern, more Western-style society and those who wanted to follow traditional Islam. Such a struggle took place in Iran. In the 1950s, a group tried to take control of the government from the shah, or ruler, who was pro-West. The United States helped the Shah defeat them.

Over time, the Shah tried to weaken the influence of the Islamic religion in Iran. A Muslim leader, the Ayatollah Ruholla Khomeini, led a successful revolt. In 1979, the Shah was forced to leave the country. Khomeini made Islamic law the law of the land and followed a foreign policy that was strongly against the United States. He also led his country to a long war with Iraq, its neighbor.

The Soviets gained influence in Afghanistan after 1950. In the 1970s, Islamic rebels threatened the country's Communist government. The Soviets sent in support troops. The United States felt its Middle East oil supplies were in danger and supported the rebels. In 1989, after a costly occupation, Soviet troops left Afghanistan.

❺ The Cold War Thaws

KEY IDEA *The Cold War began to thaw as the superpowers entered an era of uneasy diplomacy.*

When Stalin died in 1953, Nikita Khrushchev became the Soviet leader. Soon protest movements in Eastern Europe challenged the Soviets' hold there. In 1956, protesters and the army toppled the Communist government of Hungary. Khrushchev sent Soviet tanks to put the Communists back in power. Similar events took place in Czechoslovakia in 1968. That time it was new Soviet leader Leonid Brezhnev who sent the tanks.

The Soviets did not have the same control over their larger neighbor, China. Although the Soviet Union and China enjoyed friendly relations at first, they gradually grew apart.

In the early 1970s, President Richard Nixon began following a policy called détente. This was a lessening of tensions between the superpowers. He became the U.S. first president to visit Communist China and the Soviet Union. In 1972, Nixon and Brezhnev signed a treaty to limit the number of nuclear missiles each country could have.

The U.S. retreated from détente after the Soviet Union invaded Afghanistan in 1979. In 1981, Ronald Reagan, a fierce anti-Communist, became president. Then the Soviets grew angry over U.S. support for the rebels fighting Communists in Nicaragua. Tensions increased until 1985 when the Soviet Union got a new leader.

Review

Determining Main Ideas

1. What factors divided the United States and the Soviet Union?

2. How did the two superpowers tangle in the Americas?

3. ***Summarizing*** Describe the Great Leap Forward and the Cultural Revolution.

4. ***Analyzing Causes and Recognizing Effects*** Why did the United States fight in Korea and Vietnam? What were the outcomes of these wars?

5. ***Making Inferences*** How did the Soviet Union act toward Eastern Europe?

Restructuring the Postwar World, 1945–Present

Responses will vary but should include points similar to the following:

1. The United States and Soviet Union had deep economic and political differences and had come out of the war with different goals. The United States wanted to encourage democracy and trade and wanted to reunify Germany. The Soviet Union wanted to promote Communism and to take advantage of raw materials in Eastern Europe to rebuild its own economy. It also wanted Eastern Europe as a zone of defense. The Soviets wanted to keep Germany divided so it could not start another war.

2. The two superpowers first tangled over Cuba. When the Soviet Union placed missiles on the island, the United States protested. The Soviets finally withdrew the missiles. Later, when communists took control of Nicaragua, the Americans gave aid to rebels against the new government.

3. The Great Leap Forward was Mao's effort to improve the Chinese economy. It failed due to people's resentment of government control, poor planning, and bad weather, which destroyed crops. The Cultural Revolution was Mao's attempt to revive the spirit of revolution in China. Red Guards—an army of students—attacked and harassed intellectuals, scientists, and artists. The movement threw Chinese society into a shambles.

4. The United States—along with other UN nations—fought the Korean War because North Korea had invaded South Korea. After a bitter war, the two sides settled into an uneasy peace. The United States sent troops to South Vietnam to try to combat Communist rebels there. When the war became unpopular, the American government pulled out its troops. Two years later, North Vietnam conquered South Vietnam and unified the country.

5. In both the 1950s and 1960s, the Soviet Union used force to put down movements that threatened Communist control in Hungary and Czechoslovakia.

CHAPTER
18
Summary

CHAPTERS IN BRIEF *The Colonies Become New Nations, 1945–Present*

CHAPTER OVERVIEW *India and its neighbors won independence from Great Britain, but their histories have been spoiled by conflict. Many new nations arose in Southeast Asia and in Africa after World War II as colonial empires collapsed. In the late 1940s, Jewish people were given their own country in the Middle East, where fighting between Jews and Arabs has erupted many times.*

❶ The Indian Subcontinent Achieves Freedom

KEY IDEA *A number of new nations emerged from the British colony of India.*

Many Asians served in the armies of the colonial powers during World War II. The fight for freedom from Nazi tyranny deepened their desire for independence from colonial control. Also, the Japanese victories over European powers made Asian nationalists realize that the colonial rulers could be defeated. At the same time, people in Europe began to wonder if it was right for one nation to have another as a colony.

After World War II, Britain was prepared to grant independence to India—home to a large Hindu and smaller Muslim population. The British Parliament passed a law granting independence in July 1947. It created the separate Hindu and Muslim nations of India and Pakistan. The law gave people only one month to decide which country they wanted to live in and to move there. As millions of people began to move, violence broke out. Muslims, Hindus, and Sikhs—another religious group—killed each other. Leader Mohandas Gandhi pleaded to end all violence. A Hindu extremist assassinated him for protecting Muslims.

Jawaharlal Nehru became the first prime minister of India, and he led the country for 17 years. His new nation and Pakistan, however, quickly fell to war over the state of Kashmir. It bordered both countries, with a Hindu ruler and large Muslim population. Conflict over this state continues today.

Nehru tried to reform Indian society. He hoped to improve the status of the lower castes and of women. Shortly after he died in 1964, his daughter, Indira Gandhi, became prime minister. She took steps to increase food production. In 1984, she ordered an attack on Sikh rebels. A few months later, she was killed by Sikhs. She was followed by her son Rajiv Gandhi, but he, too, was assassinated

as a political protest. Separatist movements continue to disrupt Indian society.

Pakistan, too, has been marked by violence. When first formed, the nation had east and west parts that were separated by India. In a bloody fight in 1971, the eastern part won independence as the new nation of Bangladesh. Power struggles have caused turmoil in the western part since then.

Ceylon, an island on the southeastern coast of India, won its independence in 1947 as well. In 1972 it was renamed Sri Lanka. Since 1983, a Hindu minority on the island—the Tamils—have led a bloody fight to form a separate nation.

❷ Southeast Asian Nations Gain Independence

KEY IDEA *The European colonies in Southeast Asia became independent countries in the postwar period.*

In 1946, the United States gave the Philippines independence. From 1966 to 1986, Ferdinand Marcos led the country. He was elected president but after a few years ruled as a dictator. He then harshly put down dissent and stole millions of dollars from the country. When he lost an election in 1986, he refused to leave office. A large public outcry forced him to step down.

Burma was the first British colony in Southeast Asia to become independent. It changed its name to Myanmar in 1989. Since 1962, generals have ruled the country, which has often been torn by conflict.

After World War II, the British moved back into the Malay peninsula. They tried to form a country, but ethnic conflict between Malays and Chinese who lived in the area doomed the effort. In 1957, independence was given to Malaya, Singapore, and parts of two distant islands. Some years later, Singapore declared independence as a city-state.

After World War II, Indonesia became independent. The nation is spread out. It has 13,600 islands and includes people from 300 different groups speaking 250 different languages. Bringing these different people into one unified country has been difficult. In 1967, a general named Suharto took control. Many criticized him for taking over the island of East Timor and for corruption in his government. He resigned in 1998 under intense public pressure.

❸ New Nations in Africa

KEY IDEA *After World War II, African leaders threw off colonial rule and created independent countries.*

During World War II, Africans fought as soldiers along with Europeans. As a result, Africans were unwilling to suffer further domination by colonial European powers after the war.

Soon the British began letting Africans take a greater part in the colonial government of its Gold Coast colony. Kwame Nkrumah headed a movement to push for Britain to act more quickly. The effort succeeded, and in 1957 the colony became independent—the first former colony in sub-Saharan Africa. The new nation took the name Ghana.

Nkrumah had ambitious plans for building the economy of Ghana. These plans were very expensive, though, and opposition grew. Some people in Ghana criticized him, too, for the time he spent trying to form a group of African leaders. Though the Organization of African Unity was formed in 1963, Nkrumah remained in trouble at home. Finally, the army seized power in 1966 and ruled for many years.

The strong leadership of nationalist Jomo Kenyatta helped Kenya achieve independence in 1963. So, too, did an uprising of Africans called Mau Mau. This protest aimed at frightening the British settlers to leave. Kenyatta became president of the new nation. He tried to unite the many different peoples in his country. His successor, Daniel Arap Moi, had little success in governing the country. He stepped down in 2002, and a new party gained power through free elections.

Belgium granted independence to the Congo in 1960. In 1965, Mobutu Sese Seko took control. He renamed the country Zaire and ruled until 1997. Though Zaire had rich mineral resources, Mobutu's harsh and corrupt rule made it a poor country. He was overthrown in a coup in 1997, when the country's name was changed to the Democratic Republic of the Congo.

A bloody conflict for independence took place in Algeria. About 1 million French settlers lived there. They were unwilling to give up their control of the colonial government. Violence broke out in 1945 and continued for many years. In 1962, the French finally granted independence to Algeria. From 1965 until 1988, Algerians tried to modernize their country and give it an industrial economy. These efforts failed, and an Islamic party won elections in 1991. However, the government rejected the vote. Today, a deadly civil war between Islamic militants and the government rages on.

The colonies of Portugal were the last to gain their independence. In the 1970s, Portuguese troops left Angola—without putting any group in charge. Rebel groups fought a long civil war. The war stopped in 1989, but soon started again. A peace agreement in 2002 finally ended the conflict.

❹ Conflicts in the Middle East

KEY IDEA *Postwar division of Palestine made the Middle East a hotbed of nationalist movements.*

The movement to settle Jews in Palestine began in the late 1800s. These Jews believed that Palestine belonged to them because it was their home 5,000 years ago. Muslims had lived there for 1,300 years, however.

At the end of World War II, the United Nations divided Palestine in two. It left part for the Palestinian people and set aside part for Jews. Islamic countries voted against the plan, and the Palestinians opposed it. Many countries, seeing the suffering Jews had experienced in World War II, backed the idea of a separate Jewish state. On May 14, 1948, Jews declared the existence of the Jewish nation of Israel.

The next day, six Islamic neighbors invaded Israel. With strong support from the United States, Israel won the war in a few months. It also won three later wars and seized much Palestinian land.

In 1977, Egyptian leader Anwar Sadat signed a peace agreement with Israeli prime minister Menachem Begin. Egypt thus became the first Islamic country to recognize Israel. This enraged many Arabs, and Sadat was assassinated in 1981. His successor, though, kept peace with Israel.

Despite many efforts, though, Israel and the Palestinian people have not made peace. Palestinians living in Israel dislike Israeli rule. They want a nation of their own. The Palestinian Liberation

Organization (PLO), led by Yasir Arafat, became a leading group in the struggle for self-rule. During the 1970s and 1980s, the military arm of the PLO made many attacks on Israel. That nation responded by invading Lebanon to attack bases of the PLO. In the late 1980s, many Palestinian people in Israel began a revolt called the intifada, or "uprising." It lasted for years.

In the early 1990s, the two sides made some progress toward peace. Israel agreed to give Palestinians control of an area called the Gaza Strip and of the town of Jericho. The Israeli leader who signed this agreement, Yitzhak Rabin, was assassinated by a Jewish extremist who opposed giving in to Palestinians. In 2003, the two sides renewed their peace efforts with a commitment to a U.S. sponsored plan known as the "road map."

❺ Central Asia Struggles

KEY IDEA *The former lands of the Soviet Union in Central Asia struggled to become thriving nations.*

In 1991 the Soviet Union broke apart. As a result, the republics that it had conquered became fifteen independent states. These states include nine countries in Central Asia. Geographers often group these nations into two geographic areas. Armenia, Azerbaijan, and Georgia make up the Transcaucasian Republics. Uzbekistan, Turkmenistan, Tajikistan, Kazakhstan, and Kyrgyzstan comprise the Central Asian Republics.

Since independence, the countries of Central Asia have faced a number of challenges. Many of these countries were economically dependent on the Soviet Union. Thus, they have had a hard time standing on their own. In addition, hostility has arisen among some of the different ethnic groups that inhabit the area. This in turn has led to the outbreak of several regional wars.

Located just below the countries that comprise Central Asia is Afghanistan. This nation endured a long history of struggle for independence. However, it is the nation's more recent battles that have brought it much international attention.

During the 1970s, a Communist group supported by the Soviet Union sought to take control of Afghanistan. A rebel group known as the mujahideen fought the communists. The Soviets soon invaded and attempted to make Afghanistan part of their empire. Despite their superior military might,

Soviet forces could not defeat the determined Afghan guerrilla fighters. After nearly 10 years of bloody fighting, the Soviet Union withdrew.

After the Soviets left, various Afghan rebel troops fought each other for control of the country. By 1998, an Islamic group known as the Taliban controlled most of Afghanistan. The Taliban practiced an extreme version of the Islamic religion— one that many other Muslims opposed. Taliban leaders forbade women to attend school or hold jobs. They also prohibited citizens from watching television and movies or listening to modern music. Punishment for disobeying their rules included beatings and even execution.

What's more, the Taliban allowed terrorist groups to train in Afghanistan. One such group was al-Qaeda, whose leader was Osama bin Laden. Many believe this group to be responsible for the attacks on New York and Washington, D.C. on September 11, 2001.

In the wake of those attacks, the U.S. government demanded that the Taliban turn over bin Laden. The Taliban refused. Beginning in October 2001, the United States took military action against Afghanistan. By December, the United States had driven the Taliban from power. In the months that followed, Afghanis created a new government and began working to rebuild their country after decades of war.

Review

Analyzing Issues

1. What difficulties face anyone trying to make a unified country out of Indonesia?
2. Which change to self-rule do you think went the smoothest in Africa? Why?
3. *Determining Main Ideas* What type of struggle dominates the history of independence in Southeast Asia?
4. *Analyzing Causes and Recognizing Effects* Why were Sadat and Rabin assassinated?

Answer Key
Chapter 18
SUMMARY

The Colonies Become New Nations, 1945–Present

Responses will vary but should include points similar to the following:

1. Indonesia is a land of many different peoples and languages. It would be very difficult for any leader to try to unite them.

2. Several of the new nations of Southeast Asia have been caught in a struggle between democracy and the rule of a dictator or military leadership.

3. The change to independence for Ghana was the smoothest—even though the first government of Ghana was overthrown in a coup. The reason is that the British took some steps to first bring Africans into colonial government.

4. Sadat and Rabin were both assassinated by fanatics of their own ethnic groups because they dared to make peace with or compromise with their rival group.

CHAPTER

19

Summary

CHAPTERS IN BRIEF *Struggles for Democracy, 1945–Present*

CHAPTER OVERVIEW The history of Latin America revealed how difficult it is to set up a democracy. In Africa, ethnic conflicts worked against democracy. In the early 1990s, communism fell in Eastern Europe and the Soviet Union. But long-hidden ethnic tensions broke the regions into smaller countries. In China, communist leaders made economic changes but kept tight political control.

❶ Democracy–Case Study: Latin American Democracies

KEY IDEA *In Latin America, economic problems and authoritarian rule delayed democracy.*

For democracy to work, there must be free and fair elections. There must be more than one political party. The people of the country should have a good education so that they can make informed choices. They should share a common culture. All must accept the idea that everyone has equal rights. Finally, there must be rule by law, not by power. Many nations in Latin America have had difficulty achieving democracy because all these factors are not present.

In 1822, newly independent Brazil began life as a monarchy. After 1930, a dictator ruled. But, in 1956, an elected leader tried to make the economy better. He broke up large estates and gave land to the peasants. Landowners opposed the plan. They backed a group of army leaders who took power in 1964. The military ruled Brazil for 20 years. The country's economy grew, but the people had few rights. When the economy soured in the 1980s, the army gave up power to an elected president. In 2002, Luiz Inacio Lula da Silva, a leftist candidate, was elected president.

Mexico has had stable government for almost all of the 1900s. Since the 1920s, one political party—now called the Institutional Revolutionary Party (PRI)—has been in power. The PRI has controlled the local, state, and national governments. At times, the party acted harshly to stop any dissent. In recent years, though, the party has opened up the political system to candidates from other parties. In 1997, two opposition parties won enough seats to the national legislature to deny the PRI control of that congress. In 2002, Mexican voters ended PRI rule by electing Vicente Fox as president.

Argentina has struggled toward democracy, too. In the 1940s and 1950s, Juan Perón was a popular dictator. He put in place many programs to benefit the masses. In 1952, though, the army overthrew him and kept control of the government for the next 30 years. Army leaders ruled harshly, killing many who opposed them. In 1982, the army suffered a stinging defeat in a war with Britain. The generals agreed to step down. Since 1983, Argentina has been led by freely elected leaders. However, it faces severe economic problems. In 2003, Nestor Kirchner became president.

❷ The Challenge of Democracy in Africa

KEY IDEA *Recent histories of Nigeria and South Africa show ethnic and racial conflict hindering democracy.*

Nations have had a hard time setting up democracy in Africa because of colonial rule. European powers drew up borders in Africa that paid no attention to ethnic groupings. They put people who disliked each other in the same area, causing conflict. Also, they never developed the economies of their colonies. Most of the colonies lacked a middle class or skilled workers. Both are needed for a strong democracy. When Britain and France gave their African colonies independence, they gave them democratic governments. Soon, though, problems arose between rival groups.

Nigeria is an example of this. In 1960, it became independent from Britain. But conflict broke out in just a few years. The people of one ethnic group tried to break away from Nigeria but lost in a three-year civil war. After a period of military rule, Nigeria finally got an elected government. Army officers said the government was corrupt, though, and overthrew it. Once in power, they treated the people from other ethnic groups harshly. They allowed elections in 1993 but did not accept the results. In 1999, Nigerians elected their first civilian president in 20 years, Olusegun Obasanjo. He was re-elected in 2003.

In South Africa, the conflict was between races. A white minority ruled a black majority. In 1948, they put in place a policy called apartheid—the strict separation of blacks and whites. Black South Africans were denied many basic rights. Some joined together in a group called the African National Congress (ANC) to fight for their rights. The government cracked down, putting many ANC leaders in prison.

By the late 1980s, several riots had taken place, as blacks angrily struck back at the system. Also, many nations would not buy goods produced in South Africa. They hoped to persuade the government to end apartheid. In 1990, new President F. W. de Klerk took that step. He made the ANC legal and released ANC leader Nelson Mandela from prison. Parliament passed a law ending apartheid. In April 1994, all South Africans—even blacks—were able to vote in an election for a new leader. The ANC and Mandela won easily. In 1996, the new government approved a new constitution. It gave equal rights to all South Africans. In 1999, ANC official Thabo Mbeki won election as president.

❸ The Collapse of the Soviet Union

KEY IDEA *Soviet leaders Mikhail Gorbachev, Boris Yeltsin, and Vladimir Putin promoted democratic reforms and economic restructuring.*

During the 1960s and 1970s, the leaders of the Soviet Union kept tight control on society. In 1985, Communist Party leaders named Mikhail Gorbachev as the leader of the Soviet Union. He was the youngest Soviet leader since Joseph Stalin. He was expected to make minor reforms. Instead, he launched a revolution.

Gorbachev felt that Soviet society could not improve without the free flow of ideas and information. He started a policy called glasnost, or openness. He opened churches and released dissenters from prison. He allowed books to be published that in the past had been banned. Then he began a new policy called perestroika, or restructuring. It aimed at making the Soviet economy perform better by lifting the tight control on all managers and workers. In 1987, he opened up the political system by allowing the Soviet people to elect representatives to a legislature. Finally, Gorbachev changed Soviet foreign policy. He moved to end the arms race.

People from many different ethnic groups in the Soviet Union began calling for the right to have their own nation. In 1990, Lithuania declared itself independent. Gorbachev sent troops, and they fired on a civilian crowd, killing a few people. This action and lack of reform cost Gorbachev support among the Soviet people.

Many people began to support Boris Yeltsin. Old-time communists, at the same time, were becoming angrier at Gorbachev's changes. They thought the changes made the Soviet Union weaker. In August 1991, they tried to take control of the government. Thousands rallied in the streets. When the army refused to back the coup leaders, they gave up.

To strike back the parliament voted to ban the party from any political activity. Meanwhile, more and more republics in the Soviet Union declared their independence. By the end of 1991, Gorbachev announced that the Soviet Union would no longer exist. Russia and the other 14 republics were each becoming independent states.

Gorbachev lost all power, and Yeltsin became president of Russia. He faced many problems. Efforts to move the Russian economy toward capitalism caused suffering. In addition, rebels in the small republic of Chechnya declared their independence from Russia. Yeltsin refused to allow it. He sent thousands of troops, who were caught in a bloody war for two years. In 2000, Vladimir Putin was elected president of Russia and dealt forcefully with the rebellion in Chechnya, but the fighting dragged on. Putin also dealt with economic, political, and social problems in Russia.

❹ Changes in Central and Eastern Europe

Key Idea *Soviet Reforms of the late 1980s brought big changes to Central and Eastern Europe.*

Gorbachev urged leaders in Central and Eastern Europe to change their policies. They resisted, but the people of their countries wanted reform. Protest movements began to build. In Poland, many years of economic problems led the government to lift a ban on a workers' movement called Solidarity. Facing growing unrest, the government was forced to allow elections. The Polish people voted overwhelmingly against the communists and for Solidarity. However, the Polish people became frustrated with how long and painful the process was to achieve democracy and capitalism. In elections in 1995, they voted the former leader of

Solidarity out as president of Poland and elected Aleksander Kwasniewski in his place. In Hungary, reformers took over the communist party. Then it voted itself out of existence.

Change soon came to East Germany. Its leaders resisted at first. Then thousands of people across the country demanded free elections. Soon the Berlin Wall, which divided East and West Berlin, was down. By the end of 1989, the communist party was out of power. The next year the two parts of Germany, East and West, were united once again. The new nation had many problems, though. It had to fix the problems in the old East German economy.

In Czechoslovakia, similar calls for reform took place. When the government cracked down on protesters, thousands of Czechs poured into the streets. One day hundreds of thousands of people gathered to protest in the nation's capital. The communists agreed to give up power. Democracy led to a breakup. In 1993, the country split into two separate nations: the Czech Republic and Slovakia.

In Romania, a tough dictator used the army to shoot at protestors. The incident enraged Romanians. Massive protests forced him out. He was captured and executed in 1989. General elections followed.

Yugoslavia was made up of many different ethnic groups, and in the early 1990s they began fighting. When Serbia tried to control the government, two other areas declared independence. Slovenia beat back a Serbian invasion, but Serbia and Croatia fought a bloody civil war. In 1992, Bosnia-Herzegovina also declared independence. Serbs who lived in that region opposed the move. Using aid from Serbia, they fought a brutal civil war with Muslims, the largest group in Bosnia. The United Nations was able to stop the fighting, but peace remained uncertain. The change to democracy and capitalism in Central and Eastern Europe was not smooth.

❺ China: Reform and Reaction

KEY IDEA *China's government has experimented with capitalism but has rejected calls for democracy.*

Mao Zedong had tried to build a China on the ideas of equality, revolutionary spirit, and hard work. But his policies kept the economy from growing very quickly. Other leaders tried to modernize the economy. This caused Mao to launch the Cultural Revolution of the 1960s. The result was chaos, and it was followed by a period of more moderate government action.

During this time, China had little role in world affairs. Zhou Enlai, another Chinese leader, worried about this. He worked with U.S. President Richard Nixon to improve U.S.–Chinese relations.

After Mao and Zhou died in 1976, moderates took control of the government. The chief leader was Deng Xiaoping. He tried to modernize the economy. He ended farming communes and allowed farmers more freedom. He made similar changes to industry. Suddenly, people had more income. They began to purchase appliances and other goods that had been scarce before.

Deng's new plan caused problems. The gap between rich and poor grew wider, which caused unrest. Western political ideas entered the country. In 1989, thousands of Chinese students gathered in a public square in the capital of Beijing. They called for democracy and freedom. Deng responded by sending army troops and tanks to put down the rally. Hundreds were killed and thousands wounded. China has continued to stamp out protest to this day. Deng died in 1997, and was replaced as president by Jiang Zemin. Eventually Jiang retired and was replaced by Hu Jintao.

Another major issue for China was the status of Hong Kong. The island became part of China again in 1997 when the British gave it back after 155 years of colonial rule. China promised to respect Hong Kong's freedom for 50 years, but many worried.

Review

1. ***Determining Main Ideas*** In what ways do Brazil, Mexico, and Argentina show how difficult it is to establish democracy?

Identifying Problems and Solutions

2. What problems in establishing democracy occurred in Nigeria and South Africa?
3. What reforms did Gorbachev put in place?
4. ***Analyzing Causes and Recognizing Effects*** Why did the Soviet Union break apart?
5. ***Drawing Conclusions*** What path did China take, and what difficulties did it meet?

Answer Key
Chapter 19
SUMMARY

Struggles for Democracy, 1945–Present

Responses will vary but should include points similar to the following:

1. Brazil, Mexico, and Argentina all have had periods of democratic rule that have alternated with times of dictatorship. In Brazil and Argentina, problems arose because those who hold economic power resisted the actions of democratic governments. In Mexico, the problem has been that one party controlled the political process for many years.

2. In Nigeria, democracy has been hampered by ethnic conflict. In South Africa, the problem was domination by one race over another.

3. Gorbachev tried to make Soviet society more open with his policy of glasnost and tried to reform the economy with perestroika. He opened the political system to limited free elections, and he changed Soviet foreign policy by taking steps to end the arms race.

4. The Soviet Union broke apart because restless groups within it wanted their own nation and because the Communist Party had become discredited. When army leaders tried to resist the move, the people and army troops did not support their actions.

5. China took steps to make the economy more capitalistic. This led to more economic freedom, higher wages, and more consumer goods. Finally, people began to desire political freedom as well—freedoms that the government was unwilling to give.

CHAPTER 20

Summary

Global Interdependence, 1960–Present

CHAPTER OVERVIEW *New technologies have brought people around the world closer to one another and improved their lives. The world's economies have also grown closer to one another. Nations around the world have worked together to try to bring peace and end terrorism. Because of technology, the world's cultures have more influence on one another now.*

❶ The Impact of Science and Technology

KEY IDEA *Advances in technology after 1945 led to increased global interaction and improved quality of life.*

From the 1950s to the 1970s, the United States and Soviet Union took their Cold War rivalry to space. This space race also led to more global cooperation. In 1975, U.S. and Soviet spacecraft docked, or joined together, in space. Later, American and Soviet space missions included scientists from other countries. In the late 1990s, the United States, Russia, and 14 other nations worked together to build the International Space Station (ISS).

Some space missions did not include human crew members. Unmanned flights sent back pictures and information about other planets. In 1990, the United States and European countries sent the Hubble Space Telescope into orbit around the earth. This satellite continues to send back stunning images of objects in space.

Another advance in technology has been the computer. Computers have shrunk in size and grown in power since they were first invented. Consumer goods such as microwave ovens, telephones, and cars often include computer chips to keep them running. Millions of people around the world use personal computers at work or at home. Many of these people are connected through the Internet, a worldwide network of computers. The Internet allows people to access information or communicate with one another.

New technology has changed medicine as well. Surgery using lasers allows doctors to fix problems in the eye or the brain. New methods for making images of the body help doctors locate problems. Research into genes has helped unlock the secrets of some diseases.

In the 1960s, agricultural scientists started the green revolution, an attempt to increase food production worldwide. This involved the use of fertilizers, pesticides, and high-yield, disease-resistant strains of crops. The green revolution did increase crop yields. However, it had its negative side, too. Fertilizers and pesticides can pollute the environment.

Advances in genetics research seem to be helping to fulfill some of the goals of the green revolution. Resistance to pests and tolerance to poor soil are bred into plant strains, reducing the need for pesticides and fertilizers. This holds great promise for increasing food production in a world with an expanding population.

❷ Global Economic Development

KEY IDEA *The economies of nations are so tightly linked that the actions of one nation affects others.*

Technology has also changed the world's economies. In the 1950s, scientists found a new way to make plastics, which came to be widely used. In recent years, industries have begun using robots to make products. These changes have required workers to have more and different skills than before. The industrialized nations changed the focus of their economies. They came to have more jobs in service and information industries. Manufacturing jobs were more often found in the emerging nations where labor costs less.

A global economy linking the economies of different nations developed in the 1980s. In recent years, this process of globalization has speeded up. Telephone and computer links connect banks and other financial companies around the world. Multinational corporations have offices and factories in many countries. Their decisions affect workers all over the world.

An important aspect of globalization is free trade—no barriers to block goods from one country from entering another country. Many steps have been taken to put free trade in practice. In 1951, some nations in Europe joined together to create free trade among their people. That group, now called the European Union (EU), has grown to become a powerful trading block. To compete, the United States, Canada, and Mexico agreed to the North American Free Trade Agreement (NAFTA) in 1994. Organizations in Asia, Africa, Latin America, and the South Pacific have also created regional trade policies.

In recent years, there has been considerable disagreement on the impact of economic globalization. Supporters suggest that open, competitive markets and the free flow of goods, services, technology, and investments benefit all nations. Opponents charge that globalization has been a disaster for the poorest countries. Many, they suggest, are worse off today than they were in the past.

The development of the global economy has had a major impact on the use of energy and other resources. Manufacturing and trade both use huge amounts of energy. Oil has been a major source of this energy. Whenever the flow of oil has been threatened, the world's economies have suffered severe shocks.

Growth has also caused problems for the environment. Burning coal and oil has polluted the air. It has caused acid rain and brought about a general rising of temperatures on Earth. Release of some chemicals into the air has weakened the earth's ozone layer. This layer of air blocks out dangerous rays from the sun.

Many scientists understand the need to continue to let economies grow. They urge, though, that this growth take place without using up the world's resources too quickly. This movement centers on an idea called "sustainable growth."

❸ Global Security Issues

KEY IDEA *Since 1945, nations have used collective security efforts to solve problems.*

After World War II, the Cold War created new tensions among the world's nations. This uneasy situation threatened world security. So, nations began to work together to find peaceful solutions.

The United Nations (UN) was formed at the end of World War II to promote world peace. The UN provides a place for countries—or groups within countries—to speak their views. When groups at war request it, the UN can send troops as a peacekeeping force. These soldiers—who come from member nations—help stop violence from breaking out. As of 2002, the UN had 40,000 soldiers and police in 13 peacekeeping forces around the world.

Another approach to greater peace and security has been the attempt to limit weapons of mass destruction. These include nuclear missiles, chemical weapons, and biological weapons. In 1968, many nations signed a treaty agreeing not to develop nuclear weapons. In the 1990s, the United States and Russia have made agreements to destroy many of their nuclear weapons. In another treaty, many nations promised not to develop chemical or biological weapons. Threats to safety remain, however. Some nations have tried to develop and use these weapons. As a result, weapons of mass destruction continue to be a global security problem.

Another source of world conflict has been the struggle between different ethnic and religious groups. Violence has killed thousands. One effort to solve this problem has been the movement for human rights. In 1948, the UN approved the Universal Declaration of Human Rights. This statement lists specific rights that all people should have. Later, the Helsinki Accords, signed by many nations in 1975, included such rights as the freedom to exchange information. Many groups throughout the world keep a close eye on how well nations do in providing these rights for their people.

Recently, the enjoyment of a decent standard of health has become recognized as a basic human right. However, for many people across the world, poor health is still the norm. Perhaps the greatest global challenge to the attainment of good health is AIDS, or acquired immune deficiency syndrome. AIDS is a worldwide problem. However, Sub-Saharan Africa has suffered most from the epidemic. The disease has had devastating impact on the populations and economies of many countries in this region.

In recent years, millions of people have moved from one country to another. Some seek better jobs. Others hope to escape harsh treatment at home. Immigrants can bring many benefits to their new home. While people have a right to leave, every country does not have to accept them. Sometimes these people have to live in crowded refugee camps. They suffer hunger and disease and can cause political problems for the country where they are held.

❹ Terrorism Case Study: September 11, 2001

KEY IDEA *Terrorism threatens the safety of people around the world.*

Terrorism is the use of violence against people or property to force changes in societies or governments. People resort to terrorism to gain independence, to rid their country of foreigners, or to change their society. Recently, another motive for terrorism has emerged. Some people, driven by radical religious and cultural ideals, have tried to destroy what they consider the forces of evil.

The most common weapons used by terrorists are bombs and bullets. Terrorist attacks involving these weapons usually target crowded places. Some terrorist groups have used biological and chemical weapons. Others have employed cyberterrorism—attacks on information systems such as computer networks. Governments take various actions to combat terrorism. These include conducting military operations against terrorist training camps, cutting off terrorists' sources of funds, and tightening security measures at vulnerable targets.

Few areas of the world have escaped incidents of terrorism. In the Middle East, Palestinians and Israelis have argued for decades about land ownership. This argument has resulted in many terrorist acts. In Northern Ireland, the Irish Republican Army (IRA) has done terrorist acts for many years. The IRA wants the British to give up control over Northern Ireland. Terrorist groups have also been active in Asia, Africa, and Latin America.

The United States also has been the target of international terrorism. On the morning of September 11, 2001, 19 Arab terrorists hijacked four airliners, crashing them into the World Trade Center in New York City and the Pentagon in Washington, D.C. The United States responded by launching a military attack on Afghanistan, where the hijackers were trained. In addition, the United States Congress passed the USA Patriot Act, which gave the government several powers to help chase and capture of terrorists. The Congress also created the Department of Homeland Security to organize the fight against terrorism in the United States.

❺ Cultures Blend in a Global Age

KEY IDEA *Technology has increased contact among the world's people, changing their cultures.*

Changes in technology have made it possible for people to share their cultures with one another. Television is one of the main forces in this trend. Movies and radio also have had an impact in bringing the world's people together.

As a result of these mass media, the world's popular culture now includes elements from many different cultures. Popular culture includes music, sports, clothing styles, food, and hobbies. American television shows have become popular around the world. So, too, have athletes from many countries. Broadcasts of the sports events can reach millions of people in all corners of the globe.

When elements of different cultures are combined, it is called cultural blending. In recent times, ideas from the United States and Europe have been a major force in this blending. One reason is that Western nations dominate the mass media. This trend also results from the influence that the West has had in recent centuries. As a result, English is now a major world language. About 500 million people speak English as their first or second language. More people speak Mandarin Chinese. However, English speakers are more widely spread throughout the world. Western clothes can be seen throughout the world. Western foods—such as hamburgers and soft drinks—are enjoyed everywhere. Some ideas have also traveled from East to West.

Some see this growing international culture as a problem. They worry that their own culture will be drowned in a sea of influences from other lands. Some countries limit the amount of broadcast time given to foreign television programs. Others use censorship to keep unwanted ideas from entering the land. In some areas, people have revived old traditions in order to keep them alive.

Despite these difficulties, it is clear that the people of the world are more dependent on one another. All through human history, people have faced many challenges to their survival. In the 21st century, those challenges will be faced by different people around the world. They are people who are in increasing contact with others. They are people with a greater stake in living in harmony.

Review

1. *Recognizing Effects* How have computers affected the way people gather information and communicate with one another?
2. *Drawing Conclusions* How have economies changed since World War II?
3. *Identifying Problems* What problems come with economic growth?
4. *Summarizing* What efforts have countries made to increase peace and security in the world?
5. *Clarifying* Give two examples of cultural blending.

CURRICULUM

Global Interdependence, 1960–Present

Responses will vary but should include points similar to the following:

1. The system of computer networks known as the Internet allows people to gather information quickly from many different sources. The Internet also allows people to communicate with others around the world.

2. Since World War II, the world's economies have grown more tightly linked. Also, changes in technology have brought in new materials, such as plastics, or manufacturing processes, such as using robots. The nations that had industrialized first began to change their economies away from manufacturing. Those jobs went to nations that were still developing.

3. Economic growth has also led to the heavy use of world resources such as oil and to pollution, acid rain, global warming, and the shrinking of the ozone layer.

4. To increase peace, many nations have joined the United Nations, which has sent peacekeeping forces to try to end some conflicts. Many nations have also signed a treaty promising not to develop nuclear weapons, and the United States and Russia have agreed to reduce their arsenal of nuclear arms.

5. Student answers will vary but may include such phenomena as the adoption of Western clothes or fast food in Africa and Asia or the popularity of international entertainers in the United States.